INDIAN

THE HEART *of an* AMERICAN INSURGENCY

Michael Blake

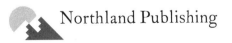 Northland Publishing

www.northlandbooks.com

Composed in the United States of America
Printed in the United States of America

Edited by Claudine J. Randazzo
Cover design by Mike Frick
Designed by David Jenney
Production supervised by Mike Frick

FIRST IMPRESSION 2006
ISBN 10: 0-87358-907-6
ISBN 13: 978-0-87358-907-9

10   09   08   07   06   8   7   6   5   4   3   2   1

Library of Congress Cataloging-in-Publication Data

Blake, Michael, 1945-
Indian yell : the heart of an American insurgency / by Michael Blake.
p. cm.
ISBN 0-87358-907-6
Indians of North America—Wars—1862-1865. 2. Indians of North America—Wars—1866-1895. 3. Indians of North America—Government relations. 4. United States. Army. Cavalry—History—19th century. 5. United States—History—19th century. 6. Unites States—Politics and government—19th century. 7. United States—Ethnic relations—Political aspects. I. Title.

E83.863.B53 2006
973.8—dc22

In memory of
JAMES ALDRICH WEBB
unpublished writer
(1947 – 2006)

Contents

My great grandfather's 1880 graduation picture from West Point. J.Y.F. Blake served with the Sixth Cavalry during the Apache Wars and knew Geronimo well enough for exchanges of gifts, one of which still exists. (Courtesy West Point Military Academy)

The Journey Back

WHILE ENROLLED AT THE UNIVERSITY OF NEW MEXICO, I perfunctorily attended class, did the reading, and took the tests.

But my real life at the university was devoted to activism and journalism. As a reporter for the daily student newspaper I sought interviews and stories that impacted the world outside what Bob Dylan once called, "The old folk's home in the college."

Occasionally, I would find myself working on stories also being covered by members of the national press. Eagerly, I compared reports in prominent magazines and newspapers to what I, too, had officially witnessed and heard.

Not one was accurate.

Whether the reporter had been sloppy or a committee of editors around a table in New York had filtered fact into falsehood, I could never discern; but that didn't matter. The appalling inaccuracies I read were disheartening to a young man who believed in the value of media. If something as basic as the number of injured was wrong, how could the rest of the article be credible?

Recorded history is plagued with the same deficiencies common in everyday journalism. But deciphering a contemporary scandal is nothing compared to the challenge of gleaning fact from fiction concerning events whose participants are a hundred years dead.

The sites still exist, and visiting these marvelous goldmines of history ignites emotion. But facts from the past are so fragile that historians, researchers, advocates, students, and teachers constantly debate, often in contention, what went before.

Custer and the Little Big Horn fight is a mighty example of the ongoing disagreements over everything that happened. Was Reno drunk? How many Indians were in combat? Was Custer hero or fool? Did Benteen dawdle on purpose? What did the Crow Scout Curly really see? The battle over answers will endure so long as that June day in 1876 is remembered.

To me, the fact that the Oglala name of the great man we know as Crazy Horse is spelled in several different ways is symbolic of how little we will ever actually know about his intimate life and those of his people. A correct spelling of his name does not even exist. Plains Indians didn't write.

Even the priceless, first-person accounts of the last, decisive battles between Indian and White are inherently flawed. Has the memory on display deteriorated with age? Could the eyewitnesses have embellished what was seen? Could personal aggrandizement be a factor? How can we know?

Even if the statement was given in a perfectly straightforward manner, it could not be accepted as pure truth. As Akira Kurosawa's film *Rashomon* so ably demonstrates, the simultaneous perceptions of those watching a drama unfold are remarkably different from one another.

Despite the excruciating dilemma of studying the past, I believe history has the capacity to provide more insight about our behavior, both as individuals and a race, than all the therapies humankind has devised.

The outstanding contributions of people like James Haley, Dee Brown, and Wilbur Nye, Mari Sandoz, Eve Ball, Stan Hoig, Alice Marriott, Ralph Andrist, Lawrence Frost, David Roberts, and many others have been instrumental in the creation of my own fictional work.

These chroniclers have provided a working knowledge of events, but the gift goes much further. Their work provokes what no dedicated novelist can do without...inspiration.

The novel *Dances With Wolves* received its initial spark of creation from an anecdote in a first-person narrative whose title and author I no longer recall. During the Civil War a freighter was delivering supplies to army posts in western Kansas. Arriving at the most remote of his stops, the driver discovered the post deserted, the only sign of life a tattered piece of canvas shifting with the breeze in the doorway of a sod hut. The driver turned his team around and started back.

But I didn't.

I imagined myself in uniform, seated next to the driver, scanning the empty post to which I had been assigned. I wondered what I would do.

From that scrap of forgotten history bloomed a saga that would come to be known and embraced throughout the world.

I have read hundreds of historically-oriented books in preparation for writing the novels *Dances With Wolves, Marching To Valhalla,* and *The Holy Road.* In some books the writing is sub-par, the facts confused, the details suspect. Other volumes have been so magnificently executed that memories of their impact are still fresh.

I have absorbed all—the poor, the mediocre, and the sublime with equal determination, always hoping that the path through known facts and salient details will lead to the revelatory realm of the intangible. It is there that figures of history become human, affording the opportunity to feel the fit of bygone shoes, run gamuts of individual emotion, suffer defeat, and celebrate victory.

My technique has been to digest masses of material before embarking on the mysterious and exhilarating process of examining the invisible treasures that lie between the lines. Imagination then discards its tethers and carries me involuntarily to a world beyond, a world where a sense of what took place begins to emerge.

In the most simple and self-serving way, all I have wanted is to be there, to witness the power of the buffalo; to interact with free-roaming tribes; to march with the troops; to fill my spirit to the brim.

What follows are conclusions I have made concerning events that occurred during what I consider one of the most poignant, instructive, and, despite enormous tragedy, most romantic periods in the history of America.

For those who revel in investigating this slice of the past much will be familiar. For those who know little much will be new. But all will view what became America's greatest insurgency through a unique lens whose light is not that of a worthy historian or academician.

This light emanates from a teller of stories whose heart and soul have been enriched immeasurably by what took place in the living West one hundred fifty years ago.

Or was it yesterday?

Or tomorrow?

Large Brule village (Courtesy Denver Public Library)

CHAPTER ONE

The Decrepit Cow

1854 FEW, IF ANY, MAMMALS ON EARTH produce less consideration from the human race than the cow. These bovine creatures are universally considered slow, brainless, and unattractive. They are slaughtered daily in numbers that are not calculable.

Yet possession of livestock is defended with the same zeal accorded a family member, and there is no example more salient than that of the cow who wandered off the Oregon Trail and into historical eternity on a late August day in 1854.

That one undistinguished animal could have ignited forty years of war, resulting in the destruction of nations, seems insane enough, but that the animal was a lame cow catapults irony into the confusing world of the surreal.

It came from an emigrant party, a convoy of people, vehicles, and animals no different from thousands of similar groups, large and small, that had been traversing Indian country for many years.

The Indians watched in astonishment as the greatest relocation of people in human history occurred across their country. Staggering numbers were made more bizarre by the fact that the hundreds of thousands of people passing before their eyes were aliens. Nothing beyond the structure of physical form was familiar to the free-roaming residents of the northern Plains.

Over time there was frequent contact between the two species, the great majority based on trade. The Whites possessed items that carried self-indulgent and utilitarian appeal for Indians, and it was the same for the White people. Disagreement and violence flared but with neither the regularity nor impact necessary to provoke war. The Indians always harbored suspicion, and among Whites, fear of Indians was practically unanimous.

Despite this profound tension, however, peace had reigned for nearly a decade.

The Mormon settler always maintained that the Indians had stolen his cow, but whether there were witnesses to corroborate his claim is not known.

Conversely, there were many Sioux who testified that the cow, emaciated to skin and bone, had appeared in the large village of Conquering Bear unannounced and, by way of sudden panic or mental defect, proceeded to stampede wildly through the camp, smashing through tipis and trampling all in its path before being killed by a visiting Minneconju named Straight Foretop. The unfortunate cow was butchered and its skimpy meat distributed, bringing to a close for the Indians a trivial and mildly amusing occurrence.

Once he discovered the fate of his pitiful possession, the owner rode immediately to the nearest army post at Fort Laramie, Wyoming. Whether he went with an entourage is not clear, but it is likely he did because the military listened attentively to the emigrant's vitriolic outrage and decided at once to support his demands for compensation.

Information has always seemed to travel through Indian ranks as if airborne. Once he caught wind of goings-on at the fort, Conquering Bear himself arrived, seeking to resolve the issue.

∾∾⚘∾∾

IN THE EYES OF THE WHITES, the chief of all the Sioux had come to talk, but that was a misperception. Indian political culture was based so intensely on democratic independence that the concept of a solitary leader was inconceivable. Peoples of various bands and families had their own leaders who were not required to follow the edicts or initiatives of others, no matter what power they might hold.

Pure democracy was an insurmountable hurdle to White negotiators, and the United States government had summarily designated Conquering Bear as president of the Sioux Nation, an act that effectively placed the designee in a vice. It was not possible to

order any Sioux about, nor was it possible to represent the whole when parlaying with the Whites.

That Conquering Bear appeared at the gates of Fort Laramie in his assigned role is testament to the confidence he must have felt in dealing with the tiny matter of the errant cow.

Commanding the small garrison at Fort Laramie was a junior officer, a first lieutenant named Fleming. Conquering Bear immediately offered ten dollars as restitution, a generous figure for a crippled cow, but the emigrant owner demanded twenty-five. Conquering Bear tried to explain that those who had killed, butchered, and eaten the cow did not possess the resources to cover such a demand. But it was already too late for any explanations.

In fact, the meeting was destined for doom from its inception. Had the opposing parties been perfectly amiable, it wouldn't have mattered. Included among the attendees was an individual whose presence would more often than not destroy attempts at conciliation in every theatre of White and Indian relations for decades to come. This human component, known as the "interpreter," and the hundreds that populated the West had but one thing in common. Their liability went unquestioned because there was no way to monitor, much less check, what the translators were saying.

At Fort Laramie, the interpreter was so obviously incompetent that many Indian groups had routinely requested he be replaced. For reasons unknown, the army retained him. Though the White interpreter was married to a Lakota woman, he knew little of the language, evidenced a mean streak, and was more often drunk than sober.

Wyuse was the moniker he went by, and in a short time his interpretations frustrated and angered Lieutenant Fleming to the point where he made the apprehension and custody of the cow killer himself a requirement for agreement. Conquering Bear told them that the cow's killer was a guest at his large Brule Sioux village, and there was no authority that could compel him to surrender.

For many years Fort Laramie, situated on the Oregon Trail, was the equivalent of a megalopolis on the northern Plains. Emigrants, soldiers, Indians, and traders all congregated at the post. The site still exists.
(Courtesy New York Public Library)

Fleming countered that Straight Foretop would be held in army custody until the White Sioux agent, who was already weeks late in arriving, appeared.

The agent was allegedly bringing annuities owed to the Sioux from a longstanding treaty. In fact, Conquering Bear and his multitudes of followers would not even have been in the vicinity when the Mormon's cow strayed off the trail had it not been for the promised and tardy provisions.

The impasse over Straight Foretop signaled the end of an already strained meeting, tainted with the confusion and misunderstanding of Wyuse's dubious translations.

Leaving the stalemate, Conquering Bear returned to his encampment on the banks of a river about eight miles south of the fort, no doubt hoping that the issue would fade into justified oblivion.

At Fort Laramie, however, perceptions were different. Lieutenant Fleming was left with the compulsion to take action over his orders being defied. It is unlikely that the issue of the cow was as trivial to Fleming as it was to Conquering Bear, for if he had anticipated the long, gory repercussions of his move, he never would have taken it.

What was more likely is that the lieutenant saw a clear-cut example of disobedience that could not be ignored, so he turned to a recent graduate of West Point, one who had often voiced his contempt of Indian behavior, to effect submission.

J. L. Grattan was so green that even his rank of second lieutenant had yet to be confirmed. Nonetheless, Fleming designated Grattan to march out in the morning with a force of twenty-nine men, proceed to Conquering Bear's village, extract compensation for the now digested cow, take Straight Foretop prisoner, and return to the post.

In addition to manpower, Grattan was granted the use of two wheeled cannons, which he ordered hauled out of the armory early the next morning. The emergence of the cannons happened to be witnessed by a Brule leader named Little Thunder who immediately carried the revelation back to the village on the river.

By the time Grattan and his expedition arrived, the sprawling village's attention was focused on the possibility of a fight. It is probable that hostilities did not erupt at once due to incredulity on the part of the Sioux. The fuss over the cow had provoked jokes and laughter throughout the camp. Now there was a small group of soldiers entering the village with wagon guns. How could such a thing be?

Wyuse was with them, and as usual, he was drunk. As the soldiers climbed out of their wagons and made a line in front of Conquering Bear's lodge, Wyuse galloped up and down, making war whoops with his hand and mouth and shouting scurrilous insults to everyone within earshot, even threatening to eat their hearts out if they did not comply with the soldiers' wishes. Wyuse's inebriation made his performance queer, and instead of feeling fury, the Sioux were still staring at the berserk interpreter in stunned

Conquering Bear was a leader caught in a classic vice. He had convinced his fol-
lowers to cooperate with a federally designated Indian agent whose inability to keep
his promises led directly to a fatal confrontation with the American Army.
Conquering Bear took the brunt of cannon and rifle fire but somehow escaped death
during the attack. A few days later, however, he died of his wounds. (Courtesy
Denver Public Library)

awe as Conquering Bear, unpainted and unclothed for war, emerged from his lodge and strode to the waiting Grattan.

The designated chief told the junior soldier that he would give up one of his own good mules to placate the emigrant. Grattan reiterated the demand that Straight Foretop be turned over. Conquering Bear responded once again that it would be impossible for him to do such a thing and, as he spoke, glanced at the open entrance of a nearby lodge.

The heavily-armed Minneconju was standing resolutely in front. Under no circumstance would he allow himself to be placed in control of Whites. A previous conflict had taken the lives of two brothers and an uncle. He would die before he would let a White man near him. From his position next to one of the cannons, Grattan dismissed Conquering Bear vehemently and stated flatly that, by any means necessary, he would have Straight Foretop in his possession.

What could have been driving young Lieutenant Grattan's impetuous, calcified thinking? He was in the midst of a huge Sioux village, surrounded by hundreds of warriors, overtly threatening violence over the death of a single cow. His vulnerability was evident to all but Grattan himself. As it would continue to be through many years to come, arrogance was a fundamental factor.

SINCE THE LANDING AT PLYMOUTH ROCK, Indians had been widely viewed as disorganized and primitive aliens who would inevitably be subverted by superior strategy and firepower. A single White fighting man was perpetually believed to be equal to scores of combative Indians, a myth that never died despite being overturned on many occasions.

But there was more at work than arrogance. There was pressure as well. Then, as now, young, low-ranking officers were caught in a terrible vice. Despite lack of experience, they were required to engender the wholesale respect of those under their command. Saddled with the same lack of experience, they were expected by their superiors to produce exemplary results. Some were able to navigate between a rock and a hard place to rise quickly to senior status. But most were not. Grattan belonged in the latter category.

Conquering Bear issued a call for families to donate horses for compensation and when five animals were committed, the chief started to turn away from the conference. At the same instant, rifles were fired from the soldier ranks, followed quickly by a blast from the cannon being manned by Grattan.

The initial barrage of lead felled a dozen or more Indians, including Conquering Bear who would die of his wounds a few days later.

The troops must have been thrilled with the damage of their first rounds, and it is hard not to wonder at the shock they felt at the moment hundreds of hardened warriors set upon them.

A blanket of Indian rage swept over them. Grattan was found with twenty-four arrows protruding from his flesh—one through his skull. Wyuse had probably left early. His body, not much more than chunks of meat, was found a quarter mile from the others. Supporting the claim that truth is stranger than fiction, one of Grattan's men, wounded mortally, not only escaped the battlefield but managed somehow to drag himself the eight miles to Fort Laramie, informing the post of what happened before he died.

Fearing a direct attack, Lieutenant Fleming huddled his remaining command behind the walls of the fort that night. Still shaky about venturing out the next day, he chose to conduct his urgent business through a pair of messengers. The first was sent to a nearby trader named Bordeaux, who was on good terms with the Sioux, asking that he retrieve Grattan's body and put the enlisted corpses in the ground.

The other courier rode east to a fort called Kearny where news of what would instantly be called a "massacre" was disseminated throughout the United States, sparking a long-running national debate about what should be done.

⊷❦⊷

THE AMERICAN ARMY had been radically downsized, but what had started with the killing of an emigrant cow would effectively begin its re-mobilization.

At the time of Grattan's death, there were fewer than two thousand soldiers stationed throughout the sprawling and enormous hunk of country designated "Indian Territory." The Grattan affair proved to those in power that troop levels would have to rise, new posts be erected, and the frontier reconfigured if the barbarians were to be punished and controlled.

This agenda was forestalled for a time due to differences of opinion. Military and civilian reports on the "massacre" flowed steadily into Secretary of War Jefferson Davis's office for several months. Some concluded that the Indians had premeditated the slaughter while others clearly blamed the young lieutenant. In the end, culpability mattered little in comparison to the desire for vengeance. Appropriations for more troops and resources sailed through Congress, enlarging the army by more than twenty percent. Included in the funding was money for the creation of an expeditionary force charged with inflicting punishment for the killing of Grattan and his men.

Secretary Davis made a popular choice in selecting General William Harney to form and lead the expedition. Harney had commanded troops in wars with the Seminoles and Mexicans and had experienced the far West. He was reputed to be a brilliant organizer at his desk and a fiery commander in the field. Standing six-feet-four-inches tall gave him an imposing presence to go with his credentials.

At Ash Hollow on Blue Water Creek, Little Thunder's band of Brules (including Spotted Tail) was attacked by a large force of U.S. soldiers in retribution for the killing of Lieutenant Grattan and his men the year before. (Courtesy Denver Public Library)

Building from the ground up with more than adequate budgetary support, Harney created a force of his own choosing and equipped it with the required weaponry. Through many fits and starts, Harney persevered and, a year later, arrived at a place on the North Platte River called Ash Hollow with a force of six hundred men.

In addition to focusing on personnel, strategy, and logistics in the months preceding, Harney had worked diligently to gather intelligence on the enemy. But once in the field, the fluid and unpredictable movements of the Indians rendered previous reports, rumors, and tips obsolete. Gathering more would be a waste, and by the time they encamped at Ash Hollow in early September 1855, Harney and his army had long abandoned all pretense of punishing the guilty. When located, any group of savages deemed hostile would be engaged.

Fresh intelligence from an emigrant train passing east brought Harney and his army to Ash Hollow. The pioneers reported to the general that several days prior a group of warriors from a nearby village had annoyed the travelers by repeatedly begging for food. When the emigrants continued to reject the Indians' request, a frustrated warrior had kicked over a coffee pot. In addition to this "hostile" action, Harney learned that the village was situated south of the Platte rather than north, a position in violation of previous agreements.

General Harney, known for his vitriol and profanity, addressed his troops on the morning of the attack, urging his command to exact murderous revenge in the name of Grattan. "Don't spare one of those damned red sons of bitches," he exhorted his men.

General William Harney near the end of his career. Known for being verbally profane and merciless in battle, his slaughter of the Brule Sioux in 1855 cemented his status. For decades afterward administrations in Washington, D.C. considered him an "expert" in Indian affairs. (Courtesy National Archives)

*Shortly after his nephew Crazy Horse's death, Spotted Tail's Brule Sioux
were moved to the Rosebud Reservation where their descendents live today.
The American government arbitrarily named Spotted Tail chief of all the
Brule and constructed a huge two-story residence for him at a cost of eight
thousand dollars. Though he neither wanted nor liked the house, it became a
symbol of his complicity with Whites. During an argument in 1881, Spotted
Tail was shot to death by a man named Crow Dog.*

(Courtesy National Archives)

Having deployed a large contingent of cavalry north of the village to cut off an anticipated retreat, Harney sent his infantry to attack from the south, but the encampment had dismantled their lodges and fled.

During the infantry's pursuit, a delegation of warriors, using an umbrella as a flag of truce, came forward to parlay. Harney granted them a few moments to state their case hoping the delay would give his cavalry more time to position themselves. The delegation was led by Little Thunder who offered a hand to Harney that was not taken.

As he had hoped, the Sioux arrested their flight while the meaningless discussion ensued. Harney demanded that all those guilty of depredations be handed over. Little Thunder responded that he lacked authority to accede to the general's demand, adding that he and his people were there now only because they had been summoned by the Indian agent from Fort Laramie. They did not want to fight.

After thirty minutes of talk, Harney again refused to take Little Thunder's offer of a handshake, instructing the Oglala leader to leave and prepare for battle.

Once Little Thunder was out of sight, Harney ordered his infantry to pursue and attack. In sight of their targets, the infantry began to fire their long-range carbines. The Sioux returned fire with old muzzle loaders, which could not reach the enemy, and the rout was on. When the foot soldiers' pursuit became exhausting, Harney's cavalry swept in from the north inflicting heavy damage.

Had Indian expertise at fighting rear-guard action been anything less than amazing, it is likely that the village of three to four hundred souls would have been obliterated. But more than half of the village escaped that day due largely to the tenacity and bravery of warriors who, outgunned and outmanned, risked all to buy crucial time for women, children, and the elderly.

For years afterwards, reports written by White fighters attested to the determination of their enemy.

Men like Iron Shell and Spotted Tail who fought side by side all day were solely responsible for saving the lives of hundreds. Spotted Tail, who in later years would achieve wide notoriety as a shrewd diplomat during Indian/White relations, was wounded four times during the hours-long fight, escaping at last on the horse of a soldier he had slain.

Though the result could have been worse, the final tally was devastating for the Sioux. Seventy women and children, many ravaged by bullets, were captured and eighty-six Sioux were killed. The normal excuse—that genders are hard to distinguish on the battlefield—was applied to blunt the fact that all but a handful of the dead were women and children who were executed as they ran or while they cringed in hiding places.

Harney organized his troops and marched them through the heart of Sioux country to Fort Pierre in central South Dakota. He had issued a summons that all tribes send delegations to a conference designed to quell hostilities. One of Harney's insistent demands impelled participants in the robbing of a mail coach and the killing of its occupants to surrender themselves, and in October of 1855 three Sioux warriors reported to Fort Laramie.

The three warriors, whose guilt or innocence was never determined, gave themselves up to get Harney and his soldiers off the backs of their people. The general ordered the three shipped to Fort Leavenworth, Kansas, where they would be imprisoned indefinitely. The Brule hero, Spotted Tail, was one of the three.

After suffering through a terrible winter at Fort Pierre that killed a huge number of horses and frostbit scores of soldiers, Harney at last succeeded in staging the peace talks in early March of 1856.

All but the northern Cheyenne were there to hear Harney warn, "We will have blood for blood," if the Indians made more transgressions. He told them that the fight against Little Thunder had been merciful, going so far as to say he had purposely let the survivors escape.

As the president's personal envoy, Harney iterated the government's basic requirements for peace; the Sioux must surrender all murderers, return stolen plunder, and keep away from emigrants traveling west. If these criteria were agreed upon the native tribes would receive the presents they had been promised, the captives from the Little Thunder fight would be returned, and the United States would protect the Sioux from White incursion.

Little Thunder himself was at the Fort Pierre meeting, and when the business of the conference was concluded, Harney offered the Brule leader his hand and said, "I will always be your friend."

THE WAR SPARKED BY A SICKLY COW WAS OVER, a conclusion endorsed by newspapers across the country. America patted itself on the back and elevated General Harney to the highest military status. In succeeding years, books would be written about his life, he would serve as a diplomat to tribes of the northern Plains, and the highest peak in the Black Hills would be named for him, as it is to this day. His wrathful and destructive temper was accepted as a quirk of personality, and his indictment as a young man for the vicious beating death of a black female slave became a non-issue.

But Grattan's death and Harney's retribution did not represent the end of anything. It only marked the beginning of nearly four decades of deceit, tragedy, and death.

It also marked the start of cultural decomposition that plagues Indian people, the

Sioux prominent among them, to this day, one hundred fifty years later.

White deceit, both in battle and council, confused and seduced the weakest elements in the bands of various tribes. Whiskey always integrated itself into the United States' gifts, turning countless warriors into alcoholics called "hang about the forts." Great numbers of Indians flocked to military posts where they indulged their addictions, lived on handouts, impressed their wives and daughters into prostitution, and betrayed their brethren whenever convenient.

The disintegration of their life way hardened those who opted for freedom, prompting a depthless alienation from those with white skin. Though not typical as an individual, Crazy Horse reflected the mass of obstinate traditionalists who refused to follow the brazen orders of a government that seemed incapable of telling the truth and showed no respect for the earth or anything else the Creator had wrought. As a teenager, Crazy Horse had witnessed the Grattan fight, and he never looked back, going out of his way to avoid Whites when he wasn't fighting back their intrusions.

Eventually, the great majority of outstanding, principled warriors died in battle or were overcome by disease. Crazy Horse held out longer than most but finally succumbed to treachery from White and Indian alike.

Between these divisions straddled a few, lonely pragmatists who correctly interpreted the handwriting on the wall and gave over their lives in the effort to make a better existence for their people under the rule of Whites.

Spotted Tail, Crazy Horse's uncle, was one of these. After rotting for a year in jail, a new United States president granted him a pardon. The distinguished warrior returned to his family and his people, but to the dismay of many, he never fought the Whites again.

When asked why, Spotted Tail inevitably made the same, one sentence reply, "There are too many."

RECOMMENDED READING:
The Long Death, by Ralph K. Andrist, University of Oklahoma Press

CHAPTER TWO

Deceit

1861

THEN AS NOW, A YOUNG OFFICER in the military is painfully vulnerable. The grunt's responsibilities are nil. Top brass can cover. Field-grade officers can pass dilemmas up and down the chain of command. Lieutenants are naked.

Young officers view great performance under pressure as their best opportunity for the upward movement that will free them from the vice. Going into the field with a mission to execute is the ultimate; a chance to distinguish and advance.

Sometimes it works. Many times it doesn't. The military craves youth and ambition, but the combination is mercurial at best and disastrous at worst. Army history is riddled with far-reaching setbacks instigated by half-baked mixtures of naiveté and zeal.

In 1861, with the country on the verge of civil war, the Southwest drew little attention from Americans. It had belonged to Mexico until 1847 and since that time, with the exception of sporadic emigrant travel, it had seen little action. The country was remote, hard, and dry. Just passing through it required above-average grit.

The region was avoided or ignored because of another factor, a human factor so imposing that it reduced White ventures into desert land to the bravest or dumbest. Aside from scattered and scratching ranchers, settlers, and entrepreneurs, the country was inhabited exclusively by a surly tribe of Indians know as Apaches.

The last of the Apache insurgents. These warriors kept the American Army frustrated for five months in 1886 and never truly surrendered. Mounted is Naiche, the son of Cochise. Standing in front of him is Geronimo. (Courtesy National Archives)

The southeast corner of what is now Arizona was the domain of what were universally depicted as the toughest of the tough…the Chiricahua Apache.

They were led by a man whose influence over his followers was unusually strong. Though he was nearing the age of forty in 1861, he was still daunting in combat, and all who met him acknowledged his intellectual ability. The Whites called him Cochise.

Like one hundred percent of his tribe, Cochise's hatred of Mexicans was profound. The Chiricahua had been raiding into Mexico for generations, and while they expected resistance to their incursions, the manner in which the resistance was mounted was based on deceit. Captured Apache women and children were sold into slavery. Warriors were plied with drink and murdered in large numbers; money was paid for Apache scalps, from elderly to infant. All of it was sacrilege to the Apache, and the contempt they had for those south of the border was fathomless.

∽∾⊱✦⊰∾∼

THE WHITES HAD BEGUN TO PASS regularly through Cochise's country with the establishment of a stage line. The Apache leader and his allies were dubious of the people they called "White Eyes" but made a practical decision concerning the new highway cutting through their homeland. They decided to let it be, even when a station was built next to the only water source for miles at the northern edge of the massive Chiricahua Mountains.

A man named James Wallace was in charge of the station, and Cochise befriended him, visiting often, teaching him the Apache language, trading services for goods, and upholding his pledge that vehicles traveling to and fro along the southern route to the West Coast would pass unmolested.

The tranquility of this arrangement was shattered forever in January of 1861 when, eighty miles away, Apache raiders absconded with twenty of a settler's cattle, and his foster son, a twelve-year-old boy named Felix.

Straightaway, the disposed cowman reported the kidnapping to the commander of an army post several miles away. The colonel at the fort accepted the stepfather's version without question, including the fateful claim that the Chiricahua, led by Cochise, had performed the reprehensible deed.

Accordingly, fifty-four soldiers, led by a recent West Point graduate, Second Lieutenant George Bascom, were organized to respond. Specifically, they were to proceed to the Butterfield Station at Apache Pass, find Cochise, recover the stolen cattle, and bring back the boy.

Upon arrival, Bascom deviously explained to agent Wallace that he was marching east but wanted to meet the famous Cochise. Wallace went to Cochise's nearby camp and told him Bascom's wish.

Known for caution, Cochise surprisingly abandoned it and arrived at Bascom's camp with two young nephews, a brother renowned as a warrior, his wife, and two small children.

Accepting an invitation to dine with the bearded lieutenant, Cochise and his family went into Bascom's tent. Once inside, Bascom's armed troops surrounded the temporary shelter.

Following the pleasantries and serving of food and coffee, Bascom shocked his important guest by demanding he return the cattle and boy he had taken. Cochise replied that he had no cattle and no White captives but offered to find out who the perpetrators might be and get back what they had taken.

Bascom ignored the offer and repeated his demand, adding that he would hold Cochise and his family hostage until the boy and cows were returned.

Pulling a knife, Cochise jumped to his feet, slashed through the back tent wall, and dashed outside. Startled at the drama of his exit, the circle of soldiers didn't fire until he was at full speed. The Apache chief sprinted in zigzags up a shrub-covered hill as fifty rounds flew past him.

One of the rounds slightly wounded Cochise, but he made it to the top and called down that revenge would be exacted for what had happened. An hour later he reappeared and called out that he wanted to talk to his brother. Bascom's troops opened fire.

Worry rose in the second lieutenant. He dismantled camp and moved to the secure rock walls of the close-by station. The next day a big band of warriors appeared on a hill above the station. Cochise was holding a flag of truce, and a parley between himself, Bascom, and a handful of backers for each was quickly arranged.

They met in the open, one hundred yards from the station. Bascom stubbornly repeated his original demand. Cochise repeated his original reply.

Monitoring from afar, agent Wallace, seeing acrimony and thinking he could have a smoothing effect, hurried impulsively toward the group discussion. He was trailed by his employees.

Cochise's watching warriors were startled to see White men suddenly rushing toward Cochise. Without thinking, they reacted to what they interpreted as an act of aggression. A group of warriors rushed out of hiding and seized the Butterfield men. Cochise and his escort ran. Bascom ordered his troops to open fire. The Apache guns spat back.

All was pandemonium. Wallace's two employees broke loose and raced for the station, but Wallace stood still and was hustled off by his captors.

The employees made it to the wall and started over it. One of them was shot to death by a fellow soldier as he dropped down. In a panic, one of Bascom's soldiers thought he might be an Apache.

The order to fire had not given Bascom protection, and he too had made a run for his life, arriving at the station with four bullet tears on his uniform, but no injuries.

That night Bascom asked his shaken men for a volunteer to ride for help. A soldier answered the call and, leading a horse, disappeared into blackness filled with Apache fighters.

BASCOM NOW KNEW that he and his men were besieged. They had little to eat and no water for their mounts. Several men had died from wounds inflicted by the Apaches, and the surviving casualties had no medicine and no doctor. Bascom kept them all cringing in fear and misery behind the station walls. Everyone expected a major attack the next day.

Instead, Cochise again appeared on a hill above the station. This time agent Wallace, whose hands were tied, was with him. The noose of a rope hung around his neck.

Cochise reiterated the appeal for the return of his family members, saying that he would trade Wallace for them, but Bascom wouldn't budge.

The outside world knew nothing of what was going on in the mountains around the station, and a wagon train coming from the west, manned by nine Mexicans and three Americans, blindly climbed into the foothills.

Soon after the wagon train had dropped down along the narrow road cutting through the pass, Cochise's warriors ambushed them. The three White Eyes were taken captive. The Mexicans were tortured and killed, and their bodies were burned along with their wagons.

Now Cochise had four captives, but he no longer cared to expose himself to Lieutenant Bascom. He had agent Wallace translate his words into a note that was to be left in plain sight for the soldiers to find. It read in part: "Treat my people well and I will do the same by yours."

Bascom found the note and read it, but he remained mute. Cochise dropped all pretense of having his family repatriated peacefully.

Though he sent out no scouting parties, Bascom and his pinned-down troops did not see any Apache for the next two days. Desperate for water, the most daring of his men spent nights crawling back and forth to the ancient springs several hundred yards away to fill canteens.

These efforts kept the soldiers hydrated enough to live, but their animals were on the brink of death from thirst. When, for a third straight day, there was no evidence of enemies in the vicinity, Bascom ordered a handful of men, possibly as few as two, to herd the stock to the nearby springs.

After the animals had drunk their fill, a mass of warriors charged out of hiding. Somehow, the soldiers escaped the attack and were able to race back to the station unscathed. But their mounts, fifty-six valuable army mules, fell into the hands of the Chiricahua.

Moments later, another large force of warriors opened a withering fire on the now-grounded cavalry embedded in the station. For days afterward sporadic firefights were conducted, but no conclusive action was taken by either side.

✂

COCHISE AND HIS MORE THAN ONE HUNDRED WARRIORS could have overrun the station and killed every White Eye. But that was not the Indian way. Warfare, from the Indian point of view, was never conducted without careful consideration of human cost. Warriors were not recruited out of population pools. A warrior was a rare commodity, an individual who had survived, since birth, the daily and dangerous rigors of a wild life to reach adulthood. Such a man could not be replaced, and the loss of even one was a powerful blow, not just to the family but also to the community at large.

Cochise decided that victory over the Whites would never compensate for the losses that would be suffered by his people. It was likely, too, that some or all of his family would die during a full-scale assault.

Unbeknownst to the Chiricahua and their new enemies, the solitary soldier who had ventured into the night succeeded in reaching safety and help. Two different detachments, from two different posts, were dispatched to rescue Bascom and his men. One of the rescue units had bumped into half a dozen warriors pushing a herd of stolen Mexican cattle to the north, not far from the scene of hostilities. The army attacked, killing three of the warriors and capturing three others. Though they were not Chiricahua, and had nothing to do with the fighting in the pass, they were carried along to the station.

Twenty-four hours later a relief force of more than a hundred troops joined the one that had arrived with the fresh captives. Bascom and his men were saved. While preparations were made to get out, military scouting parties scoured the surrounding country but could find no Chiricahua.

Cochise had departed with the arrival of the rescue parties. Negotiations had failed, as had force, and it would be futile now to take on so many soldiers. Nothing could come from conflict, and Cochise had but one option—to leave his loved ones in the hands of the White-Eyed army while he moved his people out of harm's way.

He left brutal evidence of his disgust for the Americans, evidence the troops found when they too departed the scene. Not far out of Apache Pass, the column, including Cochise's captive family and the three rustlers who belonged to the Coyotero Band, observed vultures circling high over what was obviously a food source.

On closer investigation, the soldiers discovered the bodies of four White men, mutilated so savagely that they could not be recognized. Agent Wallace was identified by the unique fillings in his teeth.

Lieutenant Bascom was no longer in charge, having been superceded by a higher-ranking officer who had arrived with the rescue party. The ravaged bodies lying before the new commander prompted him to seek revenge of his own. He declared that the six adult, male captives in his custody would be hung on the spot. To Indians (or anybody) hanging is an ignoble and creepy way to die. When told their fate, several captives lapsed into hysteria. Cochise's brother broke into a warrior's dance.

The previously intractable Lieutenant Bascom now voiced the opinion that the captives should be spared. His days in close contact with the Apache hostages might have altered his feelings, but he was overruled. The six warriors, innocent as the murdered White men, were strung up, killed simultaneously, and left to rot as their lifeless bodies hung from their respective tree limbs.

Returning to his post, Lieutenant Bascom was officially commended for his actions at Apache Pass, even though his official report, like those of the other officers, was peppered with lies, embellishments, and omissions.

Cochise's wife and children were released and made it back to their people. However, the return did little to assuage the unquenchable hatred Cochise felt over having to cut down the skeletons of his nephews and brother. For the next several months, he and his warriors, casting traditional honesty and straightforwardness aside, attacked and killed with impunity any Whites they could find in southeastern Arizona.

∾∾✱∿∿

THUS THE SEEDS WERE SEWN for twenty-five years of intermittent and hideous warfare between Whites and the Apache, all of it fueled by perpetual acts of deceit.

There was a pause with the advent of the Civil War. Forts in Arizona were shut down, and troops were deployed to other fronts. The Butterfield Road was closed, sealing off access to the Pacific Coast. The territory became a no-man's land in which Apaches, especially Cochise and the Chiricahua, ruled supreme.

Lieutenant Bascom didn't last long. In New Mexico, a year after the incident with Cochise, he was shot to death in a skirmish with Confederates.

Felix, the pre-teen whose kidnapping had set in motion the clash that would produce a quarter-century of conflict, was never found. After being raised to adulthood by his captors, he reappeared. Calling himself Mickey Free, the former captive attached himself to the U.S. Army as a translator and scout who, because of a mean temperament and chronic disloyalty, became an object of contempt for the American military and Apache alike.

Cochise continued to lead the Chiricahua in their ongoing war with Mexico and continued negotiations with Americans, meeting frequently with military and diplomatic envoys. Everyone who met him was impressed. He succeeded in establishing a reserva-

Mickey Free (back row middle) started life as a half-breed boy named Felix. His kidnapping at age twelve ignited decades of warfare that eventually destroyed the Apache Nation. In adulthood his duplicity made him an object of scorn for both Apache and White. He died homeless and indigent in twentieth century Tucson.
(Courtesy National Archives)

tion for the Chiricahua that covered most of their homeland and included an agent with whom he formed a deep friendship.

The structure was delicate, however, menaced by constant altercations between Indian and White, the ever-shifting state of American politics, and the devious agenda of Arizona residents, particularly in Tucson, who sought to keep hostilities going out of pure greed.

The relationship between the Chiricahua and the U.S. government fell apart shortly after Cochise died in 1874. Though his sons were honorable, well-intentioned men, they never came close to attaining the influence their father had possessed. The vacuum in leadership necessarily diminished the Chiricahuas' once unshakeable unity.

One warrior came to the fore who was at once a peerless fighter and a credible mystic. He hated both Mexican and American, could be shrilly annoying to his own people, and resisted to the end, becoming the most famous Apache. Today, his name is still recognizable throughout the world: Geronimo.

THE GREATEST IMPEDIMENT TO PEACE for Geronimo was the reservation system, which was implemented by ignorant and incapable American politicians. The reservation was far from the Chiricahua homeland and situated on gameless, desolate land. As usual, corruption constantly sabotaged hoped-for harmony. By far the worst aspect of the reservation structure, however, was the fact that all branches of the Apache Nation were forced to live in close proximity. It was the equivalent of forcing Catholics, Jews, Buddhists, Jehovah's Witnesses, and Mormons to worship in the same house. A moron could sense trouble in such a set-up.

With good reason, Geronimo and his followers broke out of the reservation over and over. Invariably, they would flee to the relative safety of northern Mexico where they would reside for a time before reaching a newly-framed agreement for a return to the reservation. No matter how hard they tried to assimilate, turmoil would eventually boil over, and they would take off again.

Geronimo made his last run in 1886. Most of the Apache had been subjugated, and he was able to convince a grand total of twenty-four men, women, and children to come with him. Arizonans sent up a howling that reverberated in national halls of power. The president became involved, and every stop was pulled to get two dozen Apaches back on the reservation.

A new general, known equally for self-promotion and effectiveness, was installed to oversee a mammoth military commitment. Twenty-five percent of the country's soldiers—five thousand troops—were deployed to Arizona. On the other side of the border, three thousand Mexican soldiers were pressed into action.

For five months, the twenty-five renegades successfully evaded the international army of eight thousand. Despite his limitless resources, the pompous American general could not catch the Indians, and at last, he grumpily decided to try basics. There was a man in the United States Army who was universally respected as honest and fair by the Apache. He treated them like men.

Geronimo, Natches, Son of Geronimo

ABOVE: *Geronimo leans against a wall in San Antonio, Texas, awaiting his fate. President Grover Cleveland was weighing whether to execute the great insurgent or allow him to proceed to jail in Florida. Eventually, he chose the latter option.* (Courtesy Yale Collection of Western Americana, Beinecke Rare Book and Manuscript Library)

OPPOSITE: *Geronimo mounted (left) and Naiche (right) on the Mexican side of the border, shortly before brokering an agreement that would see them join their families and friends already in prison.* (Courtesy National Archives)

The young lieutenant, Charles Gatewood, known to the Apache as "Long Nose," was elegant, educated, and pointedly disliked by the ambitious general to whom he answered. Considered too effete to be a real soldier, the general dismissed him as an untrustworthy troublemaker for previous public comments criticizing the conduct of relations with Apache people. It was the last thing he wanted to do, but the general had to assign Gatewood the task of riding into Mexico's impenetrable Sierra Madre Mountains, finding Geronimo, and bringing him back.

With the aid of two scouts who were Chiricahua, Gatewood found Geronimo. Accompanied only by a reliable translator and one or two others, Gatewood told Geronimo that the game was up. He and all the people with him would die if he didn't surrender. Understandably wary from a lifetime of experiencing treachery, Geronimo was reluctant.

Gatewood then dropped a bomb, informing Geronimo that large groups of Chiricahua had already been shipped east to captive exile in Florida. Portions of the families of his fellow renegades had gone. Geronimo's own family was gone.

Astutely, Geronimo recognized that the primary motive for resistance had been removed. He and his people traveled back to the border where he met with the general. It was at this meeting that the long circle of deceit that began with Lieutenant Bascom finally came full. A deal was struck at the council. Geronimo agreed to spend roughly two years in prison before he and his people were returned to the reservation.

A few days later the Chiricahua boarded a train and went east. The scouts went too, even those who had risked their lives to serve the army. All the Chiricahua went to prison. None would come back.

Lieutenant Charles Gatewood (Long Nose) posing in the center of the back row with his Chiricahua scouts. After months of being chased by thousands of soldiers, it was Gatewood alone who convinced Geronimo to stop running. The young lieutenant, trusted by the Apache more than any other White, was never officially acknowledged for his incredible accomplishment.
(Courtesy Denver Public Library)

A famous photo of the Chiricahua on their way to prison in the East. Geronimo and Naiche (third and fourth from the right) sit in the front row. Sixth from the right in the back row is the only known image of Lozen, likely the greatest woman warrior who ever lived. She and a large number of her comrades were installed in Alabama where she eventually died of tuberculosis.
(Courtesy National Archives)

Some were dumped in Alabama; the remainder were put in a dank Spanish fortress on the northeastern coast of Florida. Many would die of illness, but after eight years under guard and immobile, the surviving Chiricahua, Geronimo among them, boarded a train and traveled west once more.

But they did not go home. They were carried instead to a Kiowa-Comanche reservation in Oklahoma.

One night Geronimo got drunk and fell off a horse on the way to his residence. He was in his eighties. He lay passed out at the roadside through a cold winter night. When found the next morning, he was already so sick that he was taken immediately for medical care. Several days later, still officially a prisoner of war, he died.

The Chiricahua were eventually given the option of joining their Mescalero counterparts on a reservation in New Mexico. About half took the offer. The others stayed behind in Oklahoma.

Their descendents are still in both places.

RECOMMENDED READING:
Once They Moved Like the Wind, by David Roberts, Simon & Schuster

An appropriately ghostly, contemporary view of infamous Sand Creek (Courtesy Drex Brooks)

CHAPTER THREE

Wading in Gore

1864 IN HUMAN HISTORY the major flashpoint for conflict between cultures has been religion. In modern times, the U. S. military has largely gone about its business without officially invoking such incentives.

There have been exceptions. One took place in 1864, when the Cheyenne people were targeted for punishment by the citizenry of Colorado. A veteran of Civil War action, who was best known for his staunch, relentlessly zealous promotion of Christianity, was chosen to lead the force that had been assembled. What resulted was a slaughter that was not only grisly, wanton, and obscene, but that was conducted wholly without adherence to avowed Christian principles. It left the Cheyenne Indians with an inordinate distrust of Whites that fomented many more years of tragedy and remains to this day a point of enduring angst in Cheyenne tribal history.

Pitifully, the arduous event, known to history as Sand Creek, owed its origins to the unquenchable desire to strike it rich. The country had undergone a sharp economic downturn in 1857, resulting in massive unemployment. When news of a gold strike in Colorado flashed across the country in 1858, hoards of the unemployed hit the trail, marching directly through the hunting grounds of the Cheyenne and Arapahoe. The great southern herds of buffalo were centered on these grounds, and the sudden White surge disrupted them.

So eager were the gold-seekers that large numbers of the first to set out tried to make it across the Plains in winter. Inexperienced, unprepared, and ill-equipped many of the novice miners ended up owing their lives to Indians who gave the foolish White men shelter and food when death seemed sure.

The first strike proved to be a bust, as did a second. Eventually, major discoveries were made, insuring that along with the miners came farmers, retailers, bankers, educators, and organized religion.

The White mentality dictated that not only could Indian land be traversed, it could be possessed. The Cheyenne and Arapahoe took exception and conflicts rose steadily.

The dominant tribe was the Cheyenne, a people whose warriors were known for fanaticism in battle. Allied with half a dozen other tribes, the Cheyenne attacked troops, stages, and ranchers, taking advantage of every opportunity to discourage White settlement.

By the early 1860s the territory of Colorado had achieved prominence in the American landscape. Denver had reached full city status and the territory was being overseen by a gubernatorial structure that was constantly lobbying the federal government for increased support in dealing with the "Indian menace."

Though they never came to pass, Indian attacks on Denver were consistently characterized as being imminent; depredations throughout the countryside, while real, were routinely exaggerated.

For the most part, the hysterical reports from the West fell on deaf eastern ears. Whatever was happening in the territory of Colorado was miniscule compared to the predominance of the Civil War.

The territorial governor's continuous and strident pleas were finally addressed when Washington authorized him to raise a regiment that would serve the territory for one hundred days at federal expense. At the time this approval was granted, the governor issued a formal proclamation licensing all citizens to "kill and destroy hostile Indians" wherever they may be found. Years of simmering, violent hatred for Indians now boiled over into a concrete and popular desire to exterminate the free-living people of the Plains.

The governor picked a like-minded individual to command the Colorado Regiment, a man well known in the West for his success in blunting a Confederate invasion of New Mexico during the Civil War. In the same soldierly fashion, he enjoyed wide repute as an aggressive proponent of Christianity, having become a highly influential elder in the

Methodist Church after literally preaching his way to the West.

Dubbed the "Fighting Parson," his name was John Chivington and, standing more than six feet tall and weighing two hundred fifty pounds, he possessed a physique that suited his prowess as a soldier and proselytizer.

Chivington was certainly as complex as any other human, but a single characteristic stood out. He was a classic bully, and the people of Colorado happily unleashed him. The new military leader and the governor who appointed him set about at once to formulate a plan that would rid the country of Indians.

At virtually the same time, the Cheyenne and their allies were grasping at scarce opportunities to promote peace. The buffalo were disappearing before their eyes, and the majority recognized that further hostilities would only gain more death and destruction. Groups of young men, eager for status, still followed the warpath, but most elders were united in soliciting an end to conflict.

John Chivington, self-described warrior of the Almighty (Courtesy Denver Public Library)

❧❧❧

WHITES EXTENDING HANDS OF FRIENDSHIP during this period were rare, but the Cheyenne found two in the southeastern corner of what is now the state of Colorado.

The first belonged to William Bent, a trader who had been in the West since the 1830s and maintained a key stop on the old Santa Fe Trail called Bent's Fort. Bent had married a Cheyenne woman, and they had produced five children, all of whom were inclined to embrace Cheyenne culture. Two of his sons, George and Charles, had married into the tribe and were living as Indians. The elder Bent had long promoted the practicality of peace, and as hostilities escalated, he became the most prominent go-between in the region, tirelessly using his influence to close the gap between warring factions.

Just down the road was another ally, the commander of Fort Lyon, Major Edward Wynkoop. In his few months as the officer in charge, Wynkoop followed the army line. Taking orders from Colonel Chivington in the north, Wynkoop maintained a defense against the Confederate threats from the south. He also dealt swiftly and decisively with Indian depredation. But in doing his duty, Wynkoop did not desert his moral fiber and,

Camp Weld. On his own initiative, Major Edward Wynkoop brought peace-seeking leaders to Denver for a meeting with the governor of Colorado and his military co-hort John Chivington. Wynkoop kneels on the left, Captain William Soule on his right. Shortly after the inconclusive meeting, the military removed the visionary Wynkoop from the region. Soule was at Sand Creek but ordered his men not to fire. Black Kettle is directly behind Wynkoop. White Antelope sits at his right. (Courtesy Denver Public Library)

through the combative summer of 1864, came to know Indians, particularly the Cheyenne, as people. By fall of that year, Wynkoop had divested from the simple policy of killing off the enemy. In collusion with William Bent, he took a series of initiatives designed to encourage the Cheyenne to stop fighting.

Wynkoop was successful in convincing an influential leader named Black Kettle to bring his large village to the vicinity of Fort Lyon. In exchange for coming in, he offered Black Kettle army protection.

Wynkoop then took a wild step. Wholly on his own and with a column of troops, he escorted a wagon train of Cheyenne and Arapahoe leaders to Denver for a meeting with the governor and his military chief, the Fighting Parson.

Suddenly the two most prominent men in the territory, both of whom had lobbied hard for extermination, found themselves in the awkward position of having to meet with those they had publicly avowed to kill.

From the beginning of the important council, attended by the governor and a score of other dignitaries, the Cheyenne and Arapahoe professed a profound desire to stop fighting the Whites. The governor responded to these overtures of conciliation by saying that he could not make peace and that the Indians would have to place themselves in the army's custody before anything could be accomplished. To this his visitors assented unanimously, but the governor barely acknowledged their willingness to comply. Instead he began a long interrogation, demanding to know who had been responsible for the summer-long series of murders and thefts. The chiefs supplied what information they could, and the meeting concluded with Colonel Chivington declaring that so long as the Indians did not give up their arms and deliver themselves to the army he would continue to fight them.

The Indians assured Chivington that they understood and began the long trek back to Fort Lyon, satisfied that, in accepting the demands of the Whites, all would be well.

The governor's satisfaction was far more limited. He had sidestepped any formal agreement and had managed to keep his distance. But now he had a terrible problem, and Chivington, who was interested in elective office, also recognized it. The problem was fraught with danger for a politician.

In convincing the federal government to subsidize the raising of a Colorado regiment he had bombarded Congress with alarming reports of the Indian menace, going so far as to pass on unfounded rumors of war parties set to overrun Denver as fact. The Sioux had penetrated the territory from the north and the Kiowa and Comanche had made forays from the south. But these tribes were too far away for mounting offensives. If the Cheyenne and Arapahoe laid down their arms, there would be no one to fight. The hundred-day existence of the new regiment would expire without a shot being fired, and the governor would have to explain why he had taken substantial taxpayer money on what would appear to be false pretenses.

Behind the public's back, unseen mechanisms clicked into motion, producing a series of events that would make unseemly history and bring doom to the Cheyenne.

By October, the new regiment had still not taken the field. Citizens of Denver had begun to mock the operation by referring to the force as "the bloodless third" and the soldiers themselves were grumpily apprehensive. Businessmen eager to reap profits from supplying the regiment were stymied.

Near the end of October 1864, however, a sudden and decisive shift took place. Chivington saw to it that the new regiment along with three companies of an already established unit were fully furbished and took the entire force of eight hundred to a thousand men into the field.

On November 5, without warning, Major Wynkoop was relieved of his command and moved east into Kansas. A scurvy-ridden major, whose morality was widely known to be based entirely on which way the wind happened to be blowing, replaced him.

The new major told Black Kettle and the other Cheyenne leaders that he was not yet authorized to feed them and suggested they move to the Sand Creek region forty miles to the north and hunt game.

Black Kettle and his people, concerned about obtaining enough food to survive, acceded to the suggestion without hesitation, certain that they had met the White requirements for peace. A few young men were still out, but the great majority of the Cheyenne Nation had capitulated.

Bosse, Left Hand, White M...
Black Kettle, White Antelope, Bull Bear, ...
Chiefs of Arapahoe, Sioux, Cheyenne & Kiowa...

An assembly of peace proponents from various tribes. Prominent among them was the Cheyenne leader Black Kettle (second from left, front row). Miraculously, Black Kettle escaped death at Sand Creek. His Cheyenne friend White Antelope (to Black Kettle's left) was not so lucky. (Courtesy Denver Public Library)

Wynkoop left for the East shortly afterward, secure with the progress his diligent work had yielded. He had carefully laid out the current situation to his replacement and had received assurances that there would be no deviation from the plan. His own dedication to a lasting solution was evidenced by the documents he would be carrying to his superiors. One was a letter signed by all the officers at Fort Lyon, including the new major, attesting to the effectiveness of Wynkoop's policies. The other was another letter of support, this one bearing the signatures of dozens of settlers in the surrounding area whose security had been greatly enhanced by Wynkoop's efforts.

While the changes were being instituted at Fort Lyon, Chivington and his forces were combing the Arkansas River not far south. They were hoping to find and kill an elegant Arapahoe leader named Left Hand and his followers.

After several days of fruitless searching in frigid weather, Chivington abandoned the pursuit of Left Hand and led his forces north to the Santa Fe Trail. They camped at a stage stop where the officers, their commander, and several civilians enjoyed a lunch in the warmth of the station. Though they had thus far been unable to find and kill the enemy, spirits were high, especially the Fighting Parson's.

Informed that Wynkoop had been relieved, Chivington joked that the Indians had been in command, not the peace-seeking major. The diners then speculated about the scalps they would soon take, even postulating as to how the trophies might be arranged. At the conclusion of the feast, Chivington rose from his seat and professed a desire to get back to the hunt for hostiles by proclaiming, "Well, I long to be wading in gore."

When the large force arrived at Fort Lyon, the new commander expressed relief, saying he had wanted to go out himself and punish the hostiles on Sand Creek but had not had the manpower to do so.

The collective jaws of the officers loyal to Wynkoop's peace policy opened and dropped. They met first with their new commander, reminding him of the agreement made with Black Kettle, an extension of Wynkoop's initiative that had already spared countless lives, including some of their own. The replacement replied that Chivington's expedition planned to do no more than surround the encampment, recover stolen stock, and trash those who were identified as renegades.

Unsatisfied, the Wynkoop loyalists approached Chivington with their concerns. The commander was already angry about the opposition, and especially with Wynkoop's Captain, named Soule. After hearing them out, Chivington vehemently expressed his belief that it was "honorable to use any means under God's heaven to kill Indians," and the meeting concluded.

In an unprecedented move, the military peace detachment later made yet another attempt to dissuade the Christian colonel. His face dark with rage, Chivington paced the room and announced pontifically, "Damn any man who is in sympathy with an Indian."

Captain William Soule
(Courtesy Denver Public Library)

AT DAWN OF NOVEMBER 29, Chivington's forces, swollen now with troops from Fort Lyon, arrived at Sand Creek. More than a hundred Cheyenne lodges were standing on the north side of the tiny stream.

As the pony herds were cut out and captured, word spread through the village that a great force of troops was on its outskirts.

At the time there were Whites in the village, traders accompanied by soldiers, and when firing began one of the traders stuck a white flag on a pole and hurried outside but was driven back in by bullets. Being in uniform, one of the soldiers then tried. He too was driven back.

Thinking there must be a misunderstanding, Black Kettle raised an American Flag he had received at a treaty meeting in front of his lodge. It too drew fire. With no hope of reconciliation, the entire village fled for their lives.

The Cheyenne defended themselves with a few obsolete firearms and native weaponry, primarily bows and arrows. But what happened there was in many respects more grotesque than a simple rout. What happened at Sand Creek amounted to wanton evil. Chivington's final instruction to his troops that morning was, "Remember our murdered women and children." The majority of his men responded to the directive with unfeeling cruelty.

What happened over the next two days was officially reported by Chivington as a resounding victory in the face of "900 to a thousand warriors of which four to five hundred were killed." In fact, there might have been one hundred warriors who fought against overwhelming odds in a vain attempt to protect their women, children, and elderly. In actuality, fewer than fifty warriors were killed. The gross exaggeration was only the tip of falsehoods. The lack of truth was represented by all that Chivington omitted—omissions that would soon come to light.

As a sidelight to the report, Chivington singled out Captain Soule's performance as "at least ill-advised," further stating that "He (Captain Soule) thanked God he had killed no Indians, and like expressions, proving him more in sympathy with those Indians than with the Whites." The widely disseminated condemnations would have fatal consequences for the young captain. He was shot to death by a citizen who took exception to his "pro-Indian" stance.

Chivington forwarded his report to the *Rocky Mountain News* as well, and in its coverage the newspaper reported that "all had acquitted themselves well, and Colorado soldiers have again covered themselves with glory."

When Chivington and his men returned to Denver, hundreds thronged the streets to cheer them. At an intermission in a packed theatre, scores of the hundred-dayers and their cohorts appeared and were heartily applauded as they waved Cheyenne scalps in the air.

Soon, however, contradictory reports from outraged agents, civilians, and soldiers began to flood across the country, sparking a nationwide upheaval so loud that federal hearings were initiated.

Testimony was taken from dozens of participants and while a little less than half supported Chivington and his actions, the majority of evidence was rank and repulsive.

It is not hard to gauge the veracity of the testimony as it is read. Those who testified in support of Chivington were also accused of perpetration and maintained ignorance of atrocity.

It is difficult to imagine that witnesses reporting atrocities could have imagined the chilling observations they made.

It is also difficult to imagine that soldiers would testify against their brethren in uniform without being motivated by the highest principles.

At the series of hearings that bled into the following year, those who wanted to set the record straight unanimously reported that the great majority of people killed were women and their children; roughly eighty percent.

The fighting lasted from dawn until mid-afternoon, and some of what happened during that period, extracted from eyewitness testimony, follows. It is not complete but is highly representative of the bulk of testimony.

An elder Cheyenne named White Antelope advanced on the troops with upraised arms and was immediately shot down. His head was crushed and his brain leaked out. His nose and both ears were cut off. He was scalped after silver ornaments were removed from his hair. His fingers were cut apart from his hands for easy removal of his rings. His testicles were chopped off so that a tobacco pouch could be created from his scrotum.

Reading the testimony it is clear that the killing, mutilation, and defilement of White Antelope became a model for conduct throughout the attack.

When a large number of women and children, many of them infants, were found huddled in the recesses of a dugout along a cut bank, men fired into the opening. A girl of about six emerged with a white flag and was shot to death. Then the others inside were killed and mutilated.

Several soldiers chasing a group of fleeing adults noticed a toddler of about three falling behind and halted for a competition. Shots from the first two competitors missed. The third brought the child down.

A woman immobilized by bullets raised both arms for protection against a saber strike, deflected it successfully, but suffered great injury to both limbs. The soldier then left without killing her.

Prisoners were executed on the spot, including infants.

Women's chests were skinned for their breasts.

The vaginas of some Cheyenne women were cut out and used as hatbands by Chivington's hundred-day men.

Mop-up operations conducted the next day consisted of yanking half-buried bodies out of their graves and plundering them for valuables and fleshy trophies.

The village was ransacked for goods and the homes were burned.

A month after the battle, sixty-nine partial bodies were found still decomposing at the site. Many others had been buried, removed, or carried off by predators. Hundreds had been killed.

The governor, Chivington, and Wynkoop's replacement all gave testimony defending the action at Sand Creek with vague and thin excuses or simple lies.

Chivington justified the attack by swearing that fresh White scalps were found in the village and that of "five or six hundred Indians killed" he saw "but one woman who had been killed and one who had hanged herself; I saw no dead children."

The various committees, on making their reports, were direct in their condemnation of the principals.

Of the governor, one committee concluded that his testimony was characterized by the most "prevarication and shuffling" it had ever encountered and added that "he was fully aware that the Indians massacred so brutally at Sand Creek were then, and had been, actuated by the most friendly feeling toward the Whites and had done all in their power to restrain those less friendly."

The man who replaced Wynkoop was dressed down for the duplicity of watching the Indians fulfill his every demand before he "made haste to accompany him [Chivington] with men and artillery, although Colonel Chivington had no authority whatever over him."

The Fighting Parson was upbraided with obvious vitriol. "He deliberately planned and executed a foul and dastardly massacre which would have disgraced the eeriest savage among those who were victims of his cruelty."

Kit Carson, the renowned Indian fighter known for straightforwardness summed up the various findings. When asked what he thought of Chivington's and his men's conduct he called them "cowards and dogs."

No punishment was given to any of the participants. Chivington and the new major both resigned their commissions to avoid court martial.

The governor enjoyed a long, solid, and lucrative political career.

Chivington returned to Ohio where he continued to extol Christianity and made occasional speeches to supportive audiences, each marked by the declaration, "I stand by Sand Creek."

❦

THE GOVERNMENT MADE REPARATION to women and children who had survived the attack, a gesture intrinsically hollow since few women and children escaped with their lives.

Cheyenne leaders no longer had credibility when it came to promoting peace, and the frontier exploded in violence. Over the next year, the government expended thirty million dollars in troop deployment to fight outbreaks. A few dozen Indians were killed, along with hundreds of troops and hundreds of settlers. Millions of dollars in property was destroyed.

Today the Cheyenne are implanted on a huge reservation in central Montana. Its residents, as at most reservations, are plagued by unemployment, skimpy health care, and abject poverty. Their past is gone, and the future is not encouraging.

Embedded amongst these many difficulties are the everlasting words, Sand Creek. Adult Cheyenne still wince when they are spoken.

RECOMMENDED READING:
The Sand Creek Massacre, by Stan Hoig, University of Oklahoma Press

A drawing (dated around 1864) of the situation of Cheyenne tipis and the 3rd Colorado Regiment at the Sand Creek fight (Courtesy Denver Public Library)

CHAPTER FOUR

Shock and Awe

1867

DURING THE TIME that the North and South were killing each other by the hundreds of thousands, the Indians of the West enjoyed a relative suspension of hostilities.

U.S. troops were stationed in the West but in small numbers, and the lack of manpower didn't change much after the "Great Conflict" ended. People, including those in government, were sick of war and its tremendous drain of time and money, and the army was downsized to a tiny, nationwide force of about twenty thousand.

After all great wars there is a relief among humans that translates into a desire to build rather than destroy, and nineteenth century North America was no different in that regard than it is today.

The nagging question of what to do about the "Savages" was relegated to "take it as it comes" status as the United States committed itself fully to tying the country back together.

Two major railroads were at present making their way West through Kansas, and a portion of the threadbare army was pressed into service to protect and support the mammoth commercial enterprise.

As the work picked up, the Cheyenne and Sioux, whose major hunting grounds were the western half of Kansas, became increasingly enraged. Not only did the trains, their crews, and rail workers scare the buffalo, they had begun to shoot buffalo in large numbers.

A rare photograph of the elite Seventh Cavalry, trailed by supply wagons, on the march. (Courtesy Denver Public Library)

Farmers were trickling steadily into the country. Settling along waterways, they denuded the area of trees while erecting large tracts of fencing to contain their livestock. Hoping to stem the tide of invasion, the tribes began to attack settlers and railroads, a move that prompted an ever-increasing chorus for more protection.

Undermanned and undersupplied, the army came up with the plan they hoped would diminish hostilities to a tolerable level without requiring a hard-to-get increase in overall funding. It was determined that an expeditionary force would be formed to march into the heart of Indian country. The force would be large—so large that if the Indians did not bow to the might of the Whites, they could be engaged in combat with success.

A man named Winfield Scott Hancock, a general from the Civil War with a glittering record, was the widely acclaimed choice for leadership. Additionally, the Boy General, George Custer, whose name was already a household word, would bring a brand new army unit into the field to augment General Hancock's command.

Though Congress was wary of the project's cost, on paper the plan and its participants looked to be a solid investment in the development of the West. Beneath the surface, however, there were serious deficiencies. General Hancock had never been on the Plains, let alone seen an Indian. Custer had spent some time in eastern Texas but had no real experience. The new, all-volunteer army was unable to attract much in the way of quality. Many indigent immigrants whose English was poor had joined along with a significant number of criminals using the military as a hideout. Each unit had a smattering of veteran soldiers, but those who had been west of the Mississippi were scarce.

General Winfield Hancock photographed during his illustrious Civil War service (Courtesy National Archives)

The great parade of military might arrived in the heart of Cheyenne and Sioux country in early spring of 1867. General Hancock immediately announced that he was ready to have a talk with Indian leaders in the vicinity. Chiefs were summoned and Hancock did little more than accuse the people he had never met before of having White captives. The meeting ended on a sour note.

A big Cheyenne and Sioux encampment of three hundred lodges lay forty miles away, and Hancock had already announced his intention to march there and impress the Indians. Agents, and anyone else with a working knowledge of history and Indian thinking, tried to dissuade him.

Sand Creek was still fresh in Cheyenne memory, and a large military column would terrify them. They would undoubtedly flee and wreak havoc on any facilities, such as homesteads or stage stations, that lay in their path.

Hancock had already declared that "No insolence will be tolerated from any bands of Indians we may encounter," and added, "We wish to show them that the government is ready and able to punish them if they are hostile, although it may not be disposed to invite war."

At best, the impressive declaration was a muddled mission statement, aggravated by Hancock's discomfort with the country and his clear contempt for the Indians whom he regarded as unruly juveniles that needed to be taken behind the woodshed. Against the unanimous disagreement of those who knew better, Hancock assembled his long column of men and supplies and marched toward the big village.

After only a few hours, the column found itself the recipient of shock and awe. Hundreds of heavily-armed warriors suddenly appeared out of nowhere. Custer's own description captures the thrill of the moment and marks the beginning of a life-long intrigue with the wild and free people of the Plains:

We resumed the march and had proceeded but a few miles, when we witnessed one of the finest and most imposing military displays, prepared according to the Indian art of war, which it has ever been my lot to behold. It was nothing less than an Indian line of battle drawn directly across our line of march; as if to say, 'Thus far and no further.' Most of the Indians were mounted; all bedecked in their brightest colors, their heads crowned with the brilliant war bonnet, their lances bearing the crimson pennant, bows strung and quivers full of barbed arrows…in the line of battle before us were several hundred Indians, while further to the rear and at different distances were other organized bodies acting apparently as reserves.

Hancock immediately ordered his troops to form a line of battle, instructing Custer's cavalry to "draw sabers" as they galloped into position.

After what Custer described as a "few moments of painful suspense" Hancock and another general rode forward and, through a competent interpreter, sent an invitation requesting a conference.

Carrying a white flag, the great Cheyenne war leader Roman Nose advanced, accompanied by, among others, a wily Sioux named Pawnee Killer who would later exasperate Custer repeatedly.

Handshakes were exchanged and Hancock got straight to business, asking if the Indians sought war with the Whites.

Glaring at the artillery, Roman Nose replied deftly that if he and his people wanted war they would never have come this close to the big guns. Hancock then expressed his intention to continue on to the village where a more formal council could be conducted.

Roman Nose reiterated the concern that if soldiers came to the encampment the already terrified women and children would flee, adding firmly that if he wanted soldiers at his village he would have invited them.

Unimpressed, Hancock told the congregation that the march would continue and the meeting broke up; the Cheyenne and Sioux departed hastily as the troops reformed and resumed their ill-advised trek.

✌⋙✖⋘✌

LATE IN THE AFTERNOON the Indian encampment, which was hugging a beautifully forested stream, came into view, and the army went into camp close by.

In the course of a sporadic flurry of communication, Hancock learned that, true to expectations, women and children had departed. The general told a cluster of warriors that he wanted them to bring back the escapees; the men said they would need a few horses. Hancock gave them several and waited.

By nightfall he had heard nothing, and the village was still. Hancock ordered Custer to surround it with his cavalry and find out what was going on.

When his troops were in place nothing could be heard from the Cheyenne camp except the barking of dogs. Custer's interpreter called out in Cheyenne, but all he provoked was louder barking.

Fearing that his trespassing would ignite a fight from anyone still around, Custer and several others crawled on hands and knees to the closest lodge and peeked inside. The floor was covered with buffalo robes, and numerous parcels of personal belongings were neatly arranged around the home's edge. Embers still glowed in the central fire, above which hung a kettle of simmering meat that turned out to be delicious.

The three hundred lodges were empty. Hancock was incensed and wanted to torch every tipi, maintaining that this was insolence in its highest form. His own officers found the courage to suggest more patience, however, and Hancock dispatched Custer and his cavalry to pursue the Indians and bring them back.

The unwitting order would bring the Boy General to his knees over and over. Bringing back the Indians would be akin to bringing back stars, and in the process of doing so, George Custer would make serious mistakes that nearly ended his army career.

But he rode off after the Cheyenne with his trademark energy, enthusiasm, and confidence. All of that began to dissipate when, just into the pursuit, he discovered the Indians could not be tracked. Large trails shrank steadily before his eyes as the Indians scattered and disappeared into the limitless landscape.

The Smoky Hill River with a well-used road running beside it was just fifty miles north of the empty village. Mail stations serving stages, couriers, and freighters were spaced along the road, and Custer visited several to gather intelligence. The Indians had passed through with threats of violence and an attempt to overrun one of the stations.

When the new Seventh Cavalry arrived at a stop called Lookout Station they found it destroyed by fire and its three White occupants dead. They had been scalped, sliced up, and were burned beyond recognition.

Custer dispatched a report on his grisly find, and after reading it, Hancock concluded that the United States was at war. While Custer continued his mission to sweep Kansas clear of hostiles, the three hundred lodges and all they contained were set ablaze. It was later determined that the killings at Lookout were the work of the Sioux, but it was too late for a retraction, and turning all that the Cheyenne possessed into smoke insured that they would be at war for years to come.

∞≫✕≪∞

THE PLAINS DID NOT EXPLODE with Indian wrath alone. Well-meaning, hard-working agents raised a storm of protest, blaming Hancock's move for ruining years of delicate interplay. Commercial interests cried out for more protection from the already puny army, and debate in Washington D.C. began to flare over the value of the expedition, which had produced a war.

The United States' youngest general ever,
George Armstrong Custer (Courtesy National Archives)

Ardent critics accused the army of spending a million dollars a day for a conflict that had yielded not one dead Indian.

After marching more than one hundred fifty miles without engaging the enemy, Custer was forced to pull his command into one of Kansas's western forts. Spring grass had yet to appear, and without hay, his horses could not function. For more than a month, Custer stewed on the Plains, cursing the army supply system, his longtime nemesis, for its tardiness and the lame excuses that explained the delays.

The Cheyenne village had gone down in April, but it was not until June that Custer got his three hundred men and twenty wagons filled with provisions back into the field. It was then that the trickle of difficulties he had experienced to date would become an unremitting rain of woe for the young general and his charges.

The first leg of the long march, excepting the disturbing suicide of an alcoholic officer, was uneventful. Days later the command reached the Platte River in what is today southern Nebraska. At that time the river was the army's arbitrary demarcation for separating hostiles from friendlies. Friendlies were to be found north of the river. Anyone found south of it was deemed hostile.

In the shadow of a post near the Platte, Custer was reunited with Pawnee Killer, the Sioux leader he had shaken hands with on the way to the ill-fated Cheyenne village. It was an amicable meeting. Pawnee Killer expressed a fervent desire for peace, and Custer urged him to bring his followers close to the protection of the nearby post. Pawnee Killer said it would make his capitulation far easier if he could be provided with supplies, so Custer loaded him up with coffee, sugar, and a variety of other provisions.

In the meantime, the general of the army, William Sherman, had come West to make certain that Indians were being cleared to make way for the railroads and travelers to the gold fields in Colorado.

Custer was surprised when his supreme superior, at a post less than a hundred miles west, chastised him by telegram for the conduct of his meeting with Pawnee Killer.

ABOVE: *William Tecumseh Sherman, general of the army. His brutal strategies broke the Confederate back during the Civil War and he applied the same advocacy of unmitigated force to solve the "Indian problem."* (Courtesy Library of Congress)

OPPOSITE: *The Platte River, a major lifeline of westward emigrant travel and a point of demarcation during conflicts with buffalo-hunting tribes in the 1860s* (Courtesy National Archives)

Pawnee Killer, a man who stayed one step ahead during the Hancock Expedition, out-maneuvering and out-witting Custer's every move (Courtesy Nebraska State Historical Society)

Sherman said the leader and a few warriors should have been taken hostage and held until his people came under army jurisdiction.

When Sherman showed up in person, he informed Custer that Cheyenne war parties were attacking all along the Smoky Hill River back to the south. He ordered Custer to proceed in that direction and comb the intervening waterways for Cheyenne encampments. If found, warriors were to be engaged and killed, villages destroyed, women and children taken captive. Should he need supplies or fresh orders they were to be obtained from a garrison in the north.

Obediently, Custer led his column south, but now he had far more to worry about than field combat.

Army desertions had been growing steadily. The lure of quick riches at gold camps and the drain of poor rations, long, forced marches, and the amoral character of many in the rank and file had conspired to make going over the hill a tempting option. Custer's own column had been subjected to this nightmarish distraction. In one night, thirty soldiers from the Seventh had taken off, and conditions were only getting worse.

At the height of summer, Custer led his column back into unknown country. The heat was killing dogs, playing out horses, and debilitating morale. Often the column would have to go into camp without water or spend what little energy it had left after daily marches of twenty-five miles digging in dry stream beds for liquid so inundated with bitter alkali that it could barely be drunk.

The Seventh Cavalry found no hostile villages, but on a river called the Republican a large war party found the Seventh.

THE INDIANS APPEARED on a ridge above Custer's camp just out of firing range. They devoted much of a morning to taunting the troops with astonishing feats of horsemanship and hearty curses delivered in English. The mortifying displays culminated with a crude demonstration by a score of warriors who lined up, dropped their breechcloths, and, bending over, exposed their buttocks to the soldiers in the distance.

The seething troops wanted to go after the warriors, but Custer held them in check. The column was already far below full strength. Having run low on resources, Custer had deployed a group of men and wagons to the south. Though Sherman had told him to resupply from the north, Custer had decided on the advice of competent scouts that the north country would be too rugged to pass through with wagons. Being equidistant between posts, he had dispatched his relief party in the latter direction.

Splitting the difference in terms of orders, he then sent a major and ten men to the northern post to see if new directives had arrived.

Now he stood in the middle of nowhere, watching an irritating display with a reduced force. The major and his men were due back any time, and were they to encounter this large group of warriors on open ground they would be wiped out.

In addition to safeguarding his men, Custer was anxious to know what movements the Indians might be contemplating and where their village might be located. He took an action that surprised everyone, including the Indians, who had been identified as Oglala Sioux. He called for a parley with conditions that it be attended by half a dozen men from each side and that everyone be unarmed.

Meeting at the banks of the river, Custer and his entourage had carefully sequestered weapons inside their uniforms. The Indian delegation had the same idea, arriving heavily clothed despite the sweltering summer, so encumbered with concealed armaments they could barely walk.

Leading the warriors was a man with a familiar face—Pawnee Killer. The duplicitous chief was all smiles and full of friendship, but it was clear from the start that he had agreed to the council in order to get a closer assessment of Custer's strength in men and equipment.

Toward the close of the meeting, more warriors began to arrive, and when Custer took exception, Pawnee Killer said he was ready to leave. Custer said he would ride along with him to the village. Pawnee Killer made no discernable response.

As the big group of Sioux started onto the prairie Custer followed. But the heavy American horses could not keep pace with the lean, swift ponies and, once again, the Indians disappeared.

When Custer and his command returned they found their camp fully trashed. Pawnee Killer and his force had doubled back and vandalized everything they could get their hands on, tossing equipment, along with many of Custer's private possessions, into the shallow river.

This embarrassment was followed by the return of the major and his ten men whose dangerous sojourn had been for naught. No new instructions had been received.

Shortly afterward, the wandering cavalry and its commander were subjected to yet another humiliation when, at a rest stop, thirteen soldiers brazenly deserted in full view of everyone. Seven of the deserters were mounted on good horses, but six were on foot. After weeks of privation, confusion, and frustration, the Boy General blew his top, ordering three officers to pursue the men who had left on foot and shoot them.

All six of the walkers were brought back. Three were wounded (one fatally), and three were unscratched.

Sergeants informed their general that more desertions were being planned, and Custer was forced to press officers into service as night guards of their own troops. At this point, adversity in the form of new developments gang-tackled Custer's staggering column.

She was from one side of the tracks, he from the other. Her father was a judge and Republican, his a blacksmith and Democrat. After marrying, they quickly became the most famous couple in America. The Custers' union was pressured by public attention and the internal difficulties celebrity produced. Elizabeth lived another fifty-three years after Custer's death, never remarrying and never wavering in defense of his reputation.
(Courtesy National Archives)

THROUGH A ROUNDABOUT, patchwork of telegrams and messaging, words came to Custer that new directives had come into the northern post the day after the major's detachment had departed. The directives ordered Custer's column to head for an isolated post in the south, to there await more instructions. The troubling aspect of the dispatch was that the new orders had been given to a young lieutenant with ten men and a Sioux scout. The green officer had never been in the West before, and now he was searching the lethal countryside for Custer.

Morbid fears for the youngster's fate were realized on the march south when the partial skeletons of the lieutenant and his detachment were found with dozens of arrows sprouting from the corpses' rib cages. Custer ordered all in the column to watch the interment of the rotted soldiers.

No sooner had that traumatic discovery been absorbed than Custer met the wagon train of provisions he had requested coming up from the south. They had been attacked in a running fight with hostiles that lasted hours. The post in the south had also been attacked several times over the last few weeks.

But the explosions of violence weren't the worst. The deadly, incurable disease of cholera was spreading across Kansas, moving from east to west.

By pre-arrangement Custer's wife had planned to come to the very post he was now riding toward. She wasn't with the wagon train and she wasn't at the fort in the south. She was where he had left her, in the east of Kansas.

At last, the exhausted troops made it to the southern post. The fort had been under continual attack in recent weeks, and Custer wrote in his memoirs that there was little food, much of it inedible, little forage for the horses, no orders, and no medical supplies.

Custer haters (and admirers) agree that the reckless action he took next was motivated purely by a desire to get to his wife. They were physically enamored of one another, a national model of Victorian devotion, and Elizabeth Custer always served as her husband's most formidable line of support.

With an escort of seventy-two soldiers, he left his command and started east, ignoring the requirement for permission. It was a forced march, and along the way stragglers were struck by a war party. An enlisted man was killed, but Custer did not turn back to recover the body.

After riding one hundred fifty-five miles in fifty-five hours, Custer reunited with his healthy wife. A day later he was arrested and charged with being "absent from his command without authority" and "executing an unauthorized journey on private business."

Further charges were filed by a captain in the Seventh, accusing Custer of misconduct. The same captain had been dressed down by Custer in preceding weeks for being drunk on duty.

After a grueling trial that exposed raw divisions and resentment in the officer corps, the country's most celebrated soldier was convicted on all but a few charges and suspended from the army for a year without pay. Much of the country dropped its jaw in disbelief, but a significant number of politicians branded Custer's punishment not severe enough.

Custer had erred, but his fate at court-martial was heavily tainted by outside events. From early on, newspapers had characterized the expedition as a disorganized fiasco. Congress had fought all summer over the

Elizabeth Custer, photographed not long before her husband was killed (Courtesy Yale Collection of Western Americana, Beinecke Rare Book and Manuscript Library)

money being spent, one representative estimating that the blunder-filled operation would cost the nation one hundred million dollars before it ended. The pro- and anti-Indian cliques were equally disgusted.

Before Custer's trial commenced, Hancock was quietly replaced, effectively avoiding the light of scrutiny. His expedition spawned a full-scale conflict that ended with the crushing of the Cheyenne at the cost of many hundreds of lives from both sides and destruction of material goods in the millions.

∽∾⤳⤝∿∾

THROUGHOUT HISTORY, the implementation of shock and awe as a way to cow enemies into submission has been a consistent failure.

Hancock's expedition is a classic example, and its aftermath is typical. Politicians used its muddy failure for partisan attacks. Senators and congressmen, who had supported the wholly incompetent action, pointed fingers of blame at everyone but themselves and quickly returned to the business of business.

Military responsibilities were sidestepped by the highest-ranking, most politically-tied officers and were passed down the chain of command until a suitable scapegoat could be found. The resolution of Custer's culpability in a military tribunal effectively diminished the debates, accusations, and public outcry, lowering all the turbulence to a point where the military and politicians could settle back to the self-indulgent comfort of maintaining status quo.

Politicians and military leaders were intensely uncomfortable with Custer's immense popularity, and his fall gave both factions satisfaction. But the Boy General would be plucked from his pit of despair before the time of suspension expired. He was called back to the frontier, and there he stepped once again into the national spotlight with a performance so powerful that it reduced the humiliation of the Hancock Expedition to a brief, ugly footnote in the book of his life.

While White fortunes bounced up and down, those of the Cheyenne continued to descend. Hancock's razing of their largest community had produced neither shock nor awe. But it had depleted them. Thousands had lost everything but their lives, a decline that galvanized tribal hatred for Whites and turned fence-sitters into proponents for war.

There would be plenty more to come.

RECOMMENDED READING:
Bury My Heart at Wounded Knee, by Dee Brown, Henry Holt Publishing

Free-roaming buffalo, victims of the greatest slaughter in recorded history. The Indians regarded them as food sources and family members. In thirty years their numbers were reduced from a conservative estimate of twenty million to less than five hundred. (Courtesy Colorado Historical Society)

CHAPTER FIVE

Island of Rotting Horses

1868

THE BORDER BETWEEN COLORADO AND KANSAS runs for three hundred miles, cutting through the absolute heart of America's Great Plains.

Today, not much of civilization exists in the region. Most towns on the map are too small to have their population listed in back of the atlas. Some are abandoned. Some show only faint signs of life. Even the largest enclaves, boasting populations of two or three thousand, feel isolated and lonely.

Near larger centers of humanity, cows can be seen in pasture and green belts of crops indicate occasional farms. But White settlement seems feeble when compared to the vastness of the prairie pressing against its borders.

Life moves with the solemn trudge of futureless routine.

As it did when the first pioneers ventured into the region, White civilization gives the impression it is clinging to the land.

And it is.

For generations, America's Great Plains have been emptying out. The promise of cattle living off oceans of grass has never been fulfilled. Nor has the boundless harvest of agriculture. Business is static. Every year there are fewer children, fewer schools, fewer homes.

It's as if the supernatural void of earth and sky is gradually reasserting a dominance it never really lost. The dominance was only temporarily obscured by the agonizing cultural shuffle that took place one hundred fifty years ago, a bloody and numbingly tragic shift that changed the future of the place forever.

But the foundation of creation is still there. The incessant wind, the rolling prairie, the cloud world above, and the green tinted veins of water that pattern the landscape are all intact.

It is quiet now, but one hundred fifty years ago it was a very busy place, brimming with daily life-and-death exertions for survival among a people who saw themselves not as superior, but as part of the whole.

Ever-shifting rivers of buffalo streamed over the open prairies of Kansas and Colorado, a free-moving force of nature from which came the center of balance for the teeming life that surrounded them.

By 1868, however, a wave of invasion was coming, a wave that grew too fast for its height or length to be gauged by those who watched it flood over the Plains.

Whether the wave would be defeated was not an issue. It was destructive. It was everywhere. It could not be cajoled or begged or treated. It had to be fought.

∞⤬∞

THE GUT OF THE GREAT PLAINS that comprises the Kansas/Colorado border is peppered with historic sites from that time of upheaval. Some have been given designating markers by the state. Some require hikes. Some remain mysteries.

The most famous spot in the region lies forty minutes north of a stockyard town. People rarely visit because hardly any Americans know where it is, what meaning it carries, or even what it is called.

The site lies along the banks of a shallow, slow-moving stream called the Arickaree. The empty prairie slopes gradually downward on approach, bringing the traveler in sight of a lovely, green line of large and numerous cottonwood trees. They cast their shade over a few acres of rich grass next to the winding Arickaree with its clusters of bushes and reeds growing wild at its banks and on its oldest sandbars.

The place is designated a state park and lies just off a deserted two-lane road. It is possible to spend hours in the park without seeing or hearing another vehicle, which discourages all but the most adventurous and imaginative visitors who, driven by historical intrigue, position themselves for beauty and haunting.

Those who know it call the spot on the river Beecher Island, a name of irony in that it no longer exists, the forces of drought and flood having long ago rearranged or obliterated it.

The park has no information center, only picnic tables scattered under the trees. A marker etched with a few paragraphs of text informs the public of what happened where they are now standing:

In September of 1868 a group of fifty civilian "scouts" under the command of Major George Forsyth engaged hundreds of Northern Cheyenne, Sioux, and Arapahoe at this site. The Americans, trapped on a sandy island, repelled multiple assaults until, after four days, the Indians withdrew.

A relief party reached the scene and rescued the survivors. Lieutenant Frederick Beecher, second in command, was one of those killed during the siege and the conflict was named after him.

But there is far more to it than that. The words on the marker, literally set in stone, are typically one-sided and self-serving, offering a rendition of history that promotes false senses of pride, honor, and satisfaction that, instead of enlightening the public, only perpetuates its ignorance.

Evidence of this is everywhere and is no more prominently displayed than in the title: Beecher Island. Naming a conflict after an individual promotes the presumption that there was something special about the namesake's actions.

It would be natural to assume that the young lieutenant died in hand-to-hand combat, or sacrificed himself to save the group, or took an arrow in the chest dragging a bag of ammunition back to the front lines.

But nothing like that happened to Lieutenant Beecher. No doubt he was a dedicated and enthusiastic young officer. He had been on the frontier long enough to know his way around, but his time in uniform was too brief to achieve distinction.

The sole, distinguishing aspect of his participation at the Battle of Beecher Island is that he died during the enemy's first pass. Whether it was with guns blazing is unknown. It is plausible that he never knew what hit him. All anyone knows for sure is that after the enemy's initial, chaotic assault, Lieutenant Beecher was dead on the ground.

Why then was a fight that has been recounted hundreds of times in recorded history named after him? The answer lies, not in what he did, but in who he was. The lieutenant's uncle was the nationally known scholar, teacher, and writer Henry Ward Beecher; naming the battle after his nephew conveniently served the long-standing American appetite for celebrity over substance.

The fight at Beecher Island has long been celebrated as a shining example of American determination and bravery in the face of savage, overwhelming odds. But for the Whites, Beecher Island was not so much a battle as it was a humiliating ordeal that should have ended in death for Major Forsyth and his entire command. In fact, anyone who takes the time to peek under the veneer of the battle will discover that the entire foray was naïve and grossly ill-conceived. Driven by a political desire to assuage public

Major George Forsyth. He survived Beecher Island and enjoyed a long and celebrated military career, culminating with the massacre of the Sioux at Wounded Knee in 1890.
(Courtesy National Archives)

fear, the Battle of Beecher Island never should have happened. While it is connected to a long string of conflicts that, in the quick span of fifty years, brought about the displacement and subjugation of dozens of nations, Beecher Island stands today as a colorful curiosity rather than a turning point in American military history.

For the Cheyenne and their allies, however, the battle had profound, enduring consequences.

In terms of victory or defeat, the fact that they were unable to wipe out an enemy they outnumbered by more than ten to one was frustrating, but not devastating. The Indians of the Plains were seasoned in the vagaries of lethal contests. Outcomes were always delicate, and something so simple as a shifting of the breeze could turn certain victory into abject failure and vice versa.

The warriors who fought Forsyth and his scouts on the Arickaree would, in years to come, fight on in hope of somehow stemming the White tide. But after Beecher Island they would go into battle without a man whose influence, power, and skill were so revered that many regarded him as a living icon. What his precise name was or how it was pronounced is not known.

History calls him Roman Nose.

∾⊱✕⊰∾

HIS RISE AS A WARRIOR IS UNCHRONICLED, but there are absolutes that came with his ascendance. Being born in the wild and making it to teenage years was no mean accomplishment in itself. The majority of young men aspired to be warriors, but recklessness and inexperience killed inordinate numbers. Roman Nose was not among them.

Indian society was not bereft of politics. Those born to rich or prominent families enjoyed advantages from birth, and manipulating greater influence through arranged marriages and other maneuvers was commonplace. But political power held no appeal for Roman Nose. He focused entirely on warriorhood as his chosen endeavor, a field that, unlike White society, was immune to bribery, corruption, or deceit. In the world of warriors all was earned in the pure forum of the battlefield. Leaders qualified for greatness by meeting two simple criteria. They won and they survived.

Roman Nose did both.

In the years before Beecher Island he earned elite status by participating in a long string of important battles against Whites on the northern Plains, often in concert with Sioux allies. By the time the southern Plains became imperiled by White inroads, Roman Nose had gained supreme status as a war leader. His words in council carried tremendous weight and his every move was monitored. Hundreds, even thousands of Cheyenne warriors and counterparts in other tribes clamored to follow wherever he led.

By the summer of 1868 White settlement and the tentacles of the railroad had prompted increasingly aggressive reactions on the part of Roman Nose and his comrades. But it was not the roar of locomotives and the establishment of White society that troubled the Cheyenne the most. It was what transport and settlement brought with it to the southern Plains that lit the fuse of war—the flagrant, malicious genocide of the buffalo.

In the year before Beecher Island, organized hunting parties had sallied onto the prairie in large numbers, killing buffalo until their ammunition was exhausted, taking with them only hides and tongues. Rail passengers were encouraged to shoot from their windows for no other reason than to see the animals die or wander off disabled. Soldiers shot them for sport, and by mid-1868, trains filled with day hunters were traveling back and forth across Kansas.

To see animals slain in a fashion that spits on the sanctity of life, to see them staggering crippled across the prairies, and to see their intact carcasses swelling under the sun for nothing would surely create outrage in people other than Indians. But it is difficult to imagine how the Cheyenne, like many other free-roamers, must have felt. The buffalo were not simply their physical salvation. The buffalo were relatives.

The Beecher Island site on the Arikaree River photographed during a ceremony long ago. The monument inscribed with names of the American dead rises across the river in front of a copse of trees. Today the site is beautifully wooded and rarely visited. (Courtesy Colorado Historical Society, collection 10036549, ID# F3509, all rights reserved)

Fed up as the slaughter escalated, the Cheyenne of Roman Nose began to raid in dead earnest. They attacked stages and troops and occasionally trains. But the bulk of their wrath targeted the most vulnerable members of the gigantic White incursion: the settlers who hugged the region's waterways hoping to distill a living from the land.

Roman Nose led many raids along the Solomon and Saline rivers that summer of 1868, burning and killing with impunity. No White family was safe from Indian rage.

Military authority reacted by issuing orders that recalcitrant Indians were to be herded south in order to position them for incarceration on designated reservations.

The sweeping dictate immediately placed the commander of the enormous region occupied by the "hostiles" in a tight quandary. The army had been reduced to comparatively nothing following the Civil War, and the already skimpy number of troops at his disposal was tied up manning garrisons, guarding rail lines, and escorting wagon trains. Still the order had to be executed.

How he could have expected the scheme he devised to accomplish anything is not a matter of public record. Major Forsyth and Lieutenant Beecher were instructed to hire and command a force of "fifty first-class hardy frontiersmen to be used as scouts against the hostile Indians."

In both counts what hatched was ludicrous.

"First-class, hardy frontiersmen" were a myth. The majority of those who hung around the military then were career spongers, opportunistic businessmen, and criminals.

And how could fifty men to "be used as scouts" herd whole, highly-fluid nations anywhere?

Major Forsyth, a learned soldier known for toughness, recruited his fifty men and set out for "Indian country" unencumbered by wagons, tents, or cannon and outfitted with little in the way of rations.

Hoping to strike the trail of a war party, the contingent instead happened onto a much larger track, indicating a village on the move.

In a time-honored tactic of evasion, the Indians had split into smaller and smaller groups as they spread over the country. The scouts split too, sticking to a number of trails until, at last, their quarry reconverged.

The trail was now bigger than ever, and a number of scouts expressed concern that they might be biting off more than they could chew.

Forsyth countered the anxiety by reminding his force that they had been recruited to fight Indians. Otherwise, what were they doing out here? The issue did not come up again and even if it had, it would have been too late.

Why did Forsyth insist on following what was obviously a huge force with his tiny detachment? Contempt for the enemy is practically a prerequisite for opposing factions in warfare, and both Indian and White harbored plenty of disdain for one another.

But on the White side, contempt bled into a wider condemnation. Indians were widely perceived by settlers, government figures, and the military as being more animal than human. In parlays their speech was guttural, they ate with their hands, they cared nothing for money, dressed like the wild creatures they were, and in war were so disorganized that, faced with superior weaponry, they were easily scattered.

This attitude, based almost wholly on ignorance, was endemic in military circles and it was widely agreed that defeating Indians wasn't the difficulty. Catching them was the hard part.

Forsyth was an educated, former businessman who had seen plenty of action in the war between the states. By any measurement he was at least competent. Yet he subscribed to the prevailing attitude that, once found, Indians would be defeated. Odds didn't really matter.

There is no way to exaggerate the concrete quality of these perceptions held by Forsyth and most of his contemporaries. Regardless of how much knowledge was obtained about Indian life, in most minds, they remained sub-human. And no matter how many defeats American troops suffered at the hands of Indians, White arrogance never diminished.

⊷∾⊱✕⊰∽⊶

ON AN AFTERNOON IN MID-SEPTEMBER, Forsyth's command crossed from Kansas into what is now Colorado and set up camp on the grassy banks of the shallow, slow-moving Arickaree. Fortunately, they chose a site fronting a small, sandbar island, perhaps fifty feet wide by three hundred long and covered with old growth, reeds, and bushes.

Unbeknownst to them, the Indians they were following had also set up camp only a few miles downstream. They had known for days that they were being followed and by whom, and they had now decided to swoop down at dawn and kill their pursuers.

The village, consisting of several tribes and many bands, was huge by standards, and socializing was intense. Roman Nose himself had dropped in on a Sioux friend and shared food just prior to going into battle. After eating, he learned that his friend's wife had used a metal utensil in preparing the food. Such a procedure was strictly taboo, for it rendered valueless the personal medicine that Roman Nose depended on for survival in combat. Ceremonies of considerable preparation and indeterminate length would have to be conducted to right the error.

But there was no time for that, and Roman Nose, to the doubtless consternation of his followers, had no choice but to sit the battle out.

Forsyth's sentries reported the advance of the enemy, stating there were hundreds of them, and the commander made a quick decision that saved many lives. They needed a redoubt, and the only thing that might serve as one was the tiny island in the middle of the stream.

Dragging their horses and ammunition with them, the scouts made it onto the island just as their attackers came into view. The thunderous mass of riders bore straight down on the island.

The scouts opened fire with repeating rifles and pistols, far more sophisticated weaponry than their foes possessed and, while their concerted explosion of lead did not blunt the charge, the shower of bullets from the island was able to split it.

Warriors, with the exception of a few daring men who rode over the scouts, blew past the island in two streams, hanging from the sides of their horses as they fired.

Several scouts were killed on the first pass including Lieutenant Beecher. The unit's doctor was shot in the head and never regained consciousness. Major Forsyth took three bullets. One bounced off his head, leaving a permanent dent in his skull. The other two hit each of his legs. Despite his injuries, the major didn't pass out and somehow maintained command over the next four days, even going so far as to perform surgery on himself to remove a lead ball that had damaged a nerve in one of his legs.

Almost half of the scouts were disabled to some degree after the first charge, and the enemy was not going anywhere. Many warriors were taking up positions around either shore while the bulk of the fighters began to mass for another horseback assault.

Under fire from every direction, the scouts frantically dug out pits in the sand with knives, belts, and bare hands and, once settled in, took no more casualties.

The Cheyenne and their allies had lost roughly the same in dead and wounded.

The Southern Cheyenne warriors pictured here are identified as (left to right) White Antelope, Man On A Cloud, and Roman Nose. In recent years, revisionist opinion has raised doubts as to the identity of Roman Nose, but there is not hard evidence to confirm or deny his presence in the photograph. It is clear from his ornate and distinctive dress that the individual on the far right was a man of prestige and influence. His headdress is complex (as was Roman Nose's); attached to his shirt and pants are dozens of enemy scalp-locks and, as was the custom of leaders in war, he is holding a pipe. (Courtesy Colorado Historical Society, collection 10025491, ID# F5894, all rights reserved)

As always, the greatest casualties were inflicted on the horses of both sides. They were instantly marked for death, and by the end of the first hour of fighting all of Forsyth's animals were dead. The scouts couldn't move the animals that now blanketed the tiny island. Nor did they want to at first since the cover the corpses provided was essential to the survival of many. But as the day moved on, the dead began to bloat, and then to stink.

The scouts' attackers made several more charges that day without inflicting much damage. The Whites were well dug into the island, had ample ammunition, and were not going to make themselves vulnerable by running. A stalemate was building.

There was no letdown after the first assault. Hundreds of warriors continued to pour fire onto the island in hopes of killing or routing the enemy.

Neither would be accomplished, and as the day wore on, the warriors' enthusiasm began to wane. In continuing to attack an entrenched enemy, more casualties were inevitable, and a contest of attrition was not feasible. A seasoned warrior took a generation to replace; desperate as they were to repel the Whites, cost was a huge consideration. Engaging in fights only took place when odds for victory were high, and if a battle went poorly there was no dishonor in withdrawing.

At Beecher Island the odds were dropping with the sun, and by late afternoon, several disenchanted warriors rode off to find Roman Nose. He was not in camp but behind a hill near the battleground where he had sequestered himself for most of the day.

When the warriors confronted him, one openly challenged the great warrior to intervene on behalf of his brothers-in-arms, who were suffering. Whether he was moved by this challenge specifically is not known. Roman Nose's physique (he was more than six feet tall and well proportioned) was a good reflection of his immovable mentality, and it seems unlikely that the pleas of a single man or even a delegation could have pushed him. But the beseeching of that afternoon probably had the effect of a last chop at a tree that needed only one more to fall.

∽∾⤳✕⤶∽∾

HIS AGONY OVER NOT BEING ABLE TO ENTER THE FIGHT must have grown as the day progressed. The unsuccessful charges he was hearing about would have vexed a man of Roman Nose's caliber. To his mind, strong leadership would have produced a different result. He could have provided that.

In a deeper, more personal way, sitting out the fight would have grated on him as a missed opportunity. To die in bed or by accident on a hunt was a warrior's constant nightmare. Dying on the battlefield attained what could be gotten by no other means…eternal satisfaction. It was every warrior's dream, and despite his unique status, Roman Nose was like any other warrior when it came to that particular dream.

When he was confronted behind the hill, Roman Nose made no verbal response. He turned away and began to apply paint to his face. He lifted a bonnet of feathers and horns to his head, the same bonnet he had worn through all his fierce battles. He rode down to his fellow warriors and said he would now lead them. In the last charge, as had always been his practice, Roman Nose galloped yards in front of his followers.

When he reached the island he rode over an ambuscade manned by several scouts. One of them popped up and shot him in the back, the bullet entering his spine below the hips.

Roman Nose was carried back to the temporary village where he refused medical help, purportedly saying that while death was not a problem, he didn't want to live like he was now, paralyzed from the waist down. He died that night.

The next morning his wife and others took the body far out on the prairie, erected a scaffold, and placed his corpse on top.

The same night Roman Nose died, Major Forsyth called for volunteers and sent two men into the night, hoping they could slip past the enemy unscathed and somehow reach help. It was a long shot he had to take, but without help they were all sure to die.

The scouts chosen to somehow break out and secure aid turned out to be good picks. One was a wily man of late middle age, the other a savvy teenager. Removing their boots, the two walked backward off the island and succeeded in passing through the Indian line undetected. They escaped death at the hands of a war party by hiding under the rib cage of a decomposing buffalo and, miraculously, reached a stage station and then the nearest military post where relief parties were hastily organized and sent out.

No more charges were made against Beecher Island, but the Cheyenne and their friends did not let the scouts off easily, firing persistently at the island through all of the next days. By the third day, however, far fewer Indians were seen and sniping was sporadic. On the fourth day the scouts didn't see anybody but there was nothing they could do. They had no food, no transportation, and a score of groaning wounded they couldn't leave.

On the morning of their ninth day on the island, a cavalry unit came to the rescue and, except for a scout who died after his leg was amputated, all were saved.

News of the Beecher Island ordeal spread nationally and was celebrated publicly as a chest-thumping triumph of American tenacity and "supernatural bravery." Christian righteousness had emerged victorious in a battle against barbarism.

Major Forsyth became a significant celebrity. Though he endured headaches for the rest of his life, he was walking normally within a year and finished out a long and distinguished army career enveloped in an iconic glow provided by Beecher Island.

As usual, Indian casualties rose as the story was repeated, helping cement the idea that the clash was a devastating defeat for the Indians.

It was and it was not.

Fewer than ten warriors had been killed, and the tribes had left the battleground because none of the glory and honor that were the rewards of war could be gained by maintaining a siege.

Starving an enemy to death had no appeal. The result of warfare was important, but individual conduct in warfare was what really mattered, and the Whites on the island were no longer worth the trouble.

The Cheyenne continued the fight to preserve their way of life for several more years, but the loss of Roman Nose had a long-lasting impact. People living free on the Plains received the blow of death routinely, and once a person was gone their name was no longer spoken, perhaps as a technique to help govern grief. Roman Nose was no exception. His name was no longer uttered; his ponies were placed with him on the prairie, and the material possessions of his life were piled next to the body on the scaffold.

But he took with him more than himself and the trappings of his life. The inspiration for a nation went with him. In the future, many warriors would perform great deeds of sacrifice and survival for the common good, but none would ever exceed the magnificence of Roman Nose.

The great man who died at Beecher Island ended up like most distinguished Indian leaders—turning back to dust on the Plains. Like the others, unnamed and unremembered, he fell trying to preserve the only life he knew.

Did he have descendents and, if so, where could they be now? No one knows. But, if placing a wager were appropriate, it would be a good bet that the blood of Roman Nose runs yet in human form somewhere on the Great Plains.

For decades, White population on the prairies has been shrinking, and continues to wither. American Indian numbers continue to grow.

Perhaps it is all coming full circle. Perhaps nature will be allowed to restore some of what was destroyed. Perhaps there will come a day when a new monument will sit at the site called Beecher Island, a monument listing the names of warriors who died there, beginning with the man called Roman Nose.

RECOMMENDED READING:

Cheyenne Memories by John Stands In Timber, Yale University Press

CHAPTER SIX

The Music Freezes

1868

AFTER BEING COURT-MARTIALED and convicted of what amounted to dereliction of duty, George Custer and his wife Libbie hung around the site of the judgment for a few weeks. They stayed, by invitation, in the home of the army's second in command, the prominent and powerful General Philip Sheridan.

Sheridan was a major hero of the Civil War, a master at commanding, and, despite his scrimpy size, a ferocious fighter. He was a great admirer of and mentor to Custer.

The pugilistic general had been in the room at Appomattox, and after the end of war was officially signed, he tripped down the stairs with a souvenir for his Boy General who was waiting for him on the porch.

Sheridan was carrying a small table. He handed it to Custer, saying it was for him and his wife. It was the table on which the Union Chief, Ulysses Grant, had written the terms of surrender for his Confederate counterpart, Robert E. Lee.

Barely more than two years later Custer was humiliated by the guilty verdict, and so was the military. But Sheridan decisively demonstrated his loyalty by providing a man,

---

A contemporary photograph of the Washita battlefield. When Custer and his troops traversed this landscape in 1868 to attack the Indians who had been deemed hostile, blizzard conditions existed and the valley was covered in deep, freezing snow. (Courtesy Corbis, photo by Tom Bean)

who had just been suspended from the army for a full year, with a bed in his own house.

The dissension over the verdict, which much of the country did not support, dissipated quickly, however. The judgment was not going to be overturned, and it soon became too awkward to stay at an army post.

Custer and his wife returned to Monroe, Michigan, and set up housekeeping. Not knowing if he would ever be reinstated and without rank, income, or a job, Custer made a few stabs at entering the world of big business. But he possessed no profit-making skills, and his enormous celebrity was something the captains of commerce saw as a potential distraction.

None of his initiatives panned out, and most of his time was spent walking back and forth to the Raisin River to fish. Custer was an edgy man for whom action was the only reason to exist. Idleness was equivalent to living death, and the boring tramps back and forth to the river ate at him.

His mood swung narrowly from sullen to surly. He and Libbie began to have arguments. He received no hint of what the future held, and life, as he and his devoted wife had known it, was deteriorating before their eyes.

As the decline of their marriage and overall spirits was reaching dangerous speed, a beautiful bombshell suddenly changed the course of both lives. It came in the form of a telegram from faraway Fort Hays, Kansas, and was signed by General Sheridan.

September 29, 1868
General G. A. Custer, Monroe, Michigan.

Generals Sherman, Sully and myself, and nearly all the officers of your regiment, have asked for you, and I hope the applications will be successful. Can you come at once? Eleven companies of your regiment will move about the first of October against the hostile Indians.

Custer was on the train that night, and six days later he was with General Sheridan on the frontier, his court-martial, conviction, and suspension from the army relegated to bad dream status. Never again would it be an issue in his career.

✧✧✦✧✧

SHERIDAN'S EARLY OCTOBER OFFENSIVE didn't materialize. Custer had to work to reorganize the Seventh Cavalry, and the business of fighting Indians was far too fluid for scheduling.

By this time, in late 1868, the army was in full control of the "Indian Problem." In establishing reservations it was hoped that the arteries of emigrant travel and popular sites for settlement would be cleared of "savage residents." But the plan was not working. At best, reservations were a revolving door, and many bands of Cheyenne, Kiowa, and Comanche had never set foot on one.

Any Indian who was out of bounds had been deemed hostile and therefore attackable. This directive agreed perfectly with General Sheridan. Throughout his career, "Little Phil" had conducted battles with one goal…complete destruction of the enemy. Fighting Indians was no different. Publicly and privately, his avowed intention was annihilation. In a letter to his brother, Sheridan expressed the following:

> The more we can kill this year, the less will have to be killed the next war, for the more I see of these Indians the more convinced I am that all have to be killed or maintained as a species of pauper. Their attempts at civilization are simply ridiculous.

Custer's view was far different. From his first contact with Indians he had been intrigued. His interest in the cultures of many different tribes even changed his apparel. Starting with the coming campaign, he often entered the field wearing buckskins instead of a uniform.

In a book of memoirs published before his death, Custer made an incredible statement that reveals a depth of feeling for the enemy that no American officer has matched:

> If I were an Indian, I often think I would greatly prefer to cast my lot among those of my people adhered to the free open plains rather than submit to the confined limits of a reservation, there to be the recipient of the blessed benefits of civilization, with its vices thrown in without stint or measure.

Despite their differences, mutual devotion to the military kept Custer and Sheridan joined at the hip for years to come. Sheridan acknowledged

Unlike most of his fellow soldiers, Custer was enthralled with the West. His dress of choice was but one factor in his enthusiastic assimilation.
(Courtesy Little Bighorn Battlefield National Monument)

General Phillip Sheridan ("Little Phil") in the field. Sheridan was the primary designer of the military's Indian policy, strongly advocating the destruction of women and children ("Nits make lice") and the "Indian Commissary," the buffalo. (Courtesy National Archives)

that his protégée could be as foolish as he was brave and that he needed restraints but, when a warrior was needed to execute his plans, Little Phil looked unfailingly to the Boy General.

Sheridan had arranged his return to the army for one reason above all; he needed Custer's courage and tenacity. The summer before had been incessantly frustrating. Indian attacks on troops and settlers had been unabated, and Sheridan's field commander had been able to accomplish nothing in the way of stopping the violence. Punishing Indians was moot. The army had not even been able to catch them.

∞≫✕≪∞

CUSTER HAD BEEN CALLED BACK to lead what was then a new and innovative strategy. Sheridan wanted to try waging war in the dead of winter. At that time Indian ponies were too weak to be effective in battle, and warriors and their families usually hunkered down in their villages to wait out the cold. If hostiles could be located and attacked at the height of that frigid season, the result could reach a level of devastation that would force many free roamers to capitulate.

Custer quickly rebuilt the lagging morale of his regiment with what Sheridan described as a gift for bringing "poetry" and "romance" to warfare. His various cavalry units selected uniformly colored horses. A band was requisitioned to lift spirits on the march; an elite unit of the fifty best marksmen in the regiment was put together as a special, separate force with its own leaders; and, as usual, Custer relentlessly pounded the quartermaster bureaucracy into submission in providing adequate provisions for his troops.

Late in November of 1868, Custer and his force arrived at a temporary post called Camp Supply, in what is now the Oklahoma panhandle, which was the designated departure point for Sheridan's winter campaign.

Many prominent frontiersmen had warned Sheridan that going onto the frozen Plains could prove fatal to his soldiers, but Little Phil remained adamant in his belief. Even when the weather, already nasty, turned to full blizzard conditions, no one balked. Far from being discouraged by sub-zero temperatures, feet of snow on the ground, and a storm that reduced visibility to nothing, Custer characterized the situation as "just what we need."

Sheridan's orders were simple. Custer was to proceed south to the creek-like Washita River where many bands of hostiles were believed to have made winter camps. Any renegades encountered were to be engaged and killed and their villages destroyed. Any headmen among the prisoners were to be hung. Women and children were to be brought back.

Unofficially, Sheridan deemphasized the taking of prisoners. Since his arrival in the

West he had often stated his position concerning Indian women and children on the battlefield by invoking the commonly used expression, "Nits make lice."

Accompanied by a contingent of Osage scouts and leading seven hundred men and a wagon train of provisions, Custer took his force into the unknown at six o'clock on the morning of November 23.

Snow was blowing so heavily that the Osages were unable to see where they were going, so Custer rode into the lead, letting the barely visible compass cradled in the palm of his hand take him south.

The concept of a winter campaign appealed greatly to Custer. He could move across the frozen waste of the southern Plains undetected, and once those who had not submitted to government directives were located, he could strike them with the advantage of complete surprise.

The rub was that, after three days of struggling through snow and cold, fording ice-caked creeks, camping in the open, and battling frostbite and snow blindness, there was no sign of the enemy.

Custer's hound-like mentality was at its apex, and he did not hesitate in going from push to shove. Reveille came in darkness of the fourth day out, and before first light Custer had dispatched Major Joel Elliot with a blend of White and Indian scouts as well as three companies of cavalry to search west along a major waterway. At midday one of the White scouts returned with exciting news. A huge trail of roughly one to two hundred ponies had been discovered. It was moving from north to south, and there were no dog tracks. It had to be a war party.

Custer had instructed Elliot to follow any good trail. Now he had to catch up. Leaving eighty men to accompany the wagon train, which would follow as best it could, the dogged Boy General marched the bulk of his command west to pick up Elliot's trail. They rode for hours without stopping. At intervals the men were ordered to dismount and struggle through the deep, crusty snow so that their feet wouldn't freeze in the stirrups. Hour after hour passed, but there was no evidence of Elliot.

Custer pushed on and, finally, at about eight o'clock at night, Elliot's trail was struck. At nine p.m. they overtook the major.

The soldiers rested for an hour, after which they marched until midnight when they neared the Washita River. Custer kept going, following two of his Osage scouts. Reaching a hillside above the river, Custer peered down into the darkness and was told there was a large village just below him. Out of the blackness came a dog bark, then the tinkling of a bell. Custer listened for more confirmation but, hearing nothing, finally turned back to his troops when the faint but chillingly distinct cry of a baby reached his ears.

Certain they had not been discovered, Custer immediately formulated plans for a dawn attack.

Major Joel Elliot, Custer's second in command at the Washita fight.
Impulsively, he chased fleeing Indians and was trapped and killed with his men
a few miles south of the battle site. Custer was castigated for leaving the bodies
behind, a move that created divisions in the Seventh Cavalry that would last
for years. (Courtesy National Archives)

The Cheyenne slept in the river valley while hundreds of troops whispered above them. For some, sleep was fitful. Their leader was the famous, peace-seeking survivor of what had come to be known as the Sand Creek Massacre.

In fact, Black Kettle had just returned from peace talks with the army at a post in the East. He had been told that his only guarantee of protection would come if he moved his people close to the fort, a compromise Black Kettle was considering. But the weather had been unnavigable, and unrest was everywhere. A large war party, much of which had passed on to other villages down the river, had come in that very day. And that evening a passing Kiowa party had reported soldiers in the vicinity. Black Kettle's wife was lobbying him to move at that moment, and his sleep that night was not pacific.

He awoke at first light, dressed, and went outside.

A woman screaming, "Soldiers!" ran from the darkness as a great rumble of hooves was heard racing into the village. He hadn't heard the band sound the charge because the players' spittle froze in their instruments after a few notes.

The thunder of charging horses was one of the last earthly sounds heard by Black Kettle. Within minutes, both he and his wife were shot to death as they fled across the river.

Officially, one hundred three warriors died in combat. The Seventh Cavalry suffered twenty-one killed and fourteen wounded. Fifty-three Cheyenne prisoners were taken, the village was burned along with everything the Cheyenne possessed, and several hundred

The Washita River, a vital waterway on the southern Plains. Black Kettle's village was situated to the left of the stream when Custer's forces attacked in the pre-dawn hours of November 26, 1868. (Courtesy National Park Service)

ponies from their herd were shot. In every way, from the strategy of splitting his command so as to attack from all sides, to the final result, Custer's was a complete victory.

∽∾⤬∾∿

BUT THERE WERE ALSO MISTAKES and long-lasting repercussions, some of which would haunt the young general for the rest of his life.

Prior to the battle he had ordered that the non-combatants were not to be killed, but as the village was being cleared after the initial charge, word of atrocity came. In the midst of fighting, Custer rode to the spot where women and children were being shot and put a stop to it. In his official report, Custer was one of the few commanders ever to admit that his troops had killed women and children.

Early in the battle, Major Elliot spotted a large group of women and youngsters running away, and with sixteen men, he galloped out of the village in pursuit. As he raced off, Elliot called to one of his fellow officers, "Here goes for a brevet [field promotion] or a coffin." The field promotion never came, but the coffin did.

When Custer was informed of Elliot's action, he sent out a scouting party to locate the overdue major. The scouts traveled two miles south of the village but found nothing and turned back.

By this time the battle was over, but Custer suddenly faced a challenge larger than having men missing in the field. While mop-up operations continued, the bluffs around the valley were filling with mounted warriors. Through interrogating captives, Custer discovered that villages of more Cheyenne, Arapahoe, and Kiowa hugged the river for miles to the south.

There were thousands of Indians in close proximity, and hundreds of fighters were surrounding the village he now occupied. The lagging wagon train loaded with critical provisions was somewhere on the prairie now cut off by the rapidly assembling warriors from downstream.

Whether it was born by Custer alone or in part by consultations with his scouts and officers, the next move was brilliant. Custer formed his hundreds of men into marching order and started south toward the unscathed villages.

The warriors who had surrounded them were soon in full flight, intent on reaching and protecting their families. As soon as the mass of Indian fighters had dispersed, Custer called a halt, about-faced, and countermarched back to Black Kettle's ruined village. From there the Seventh successfully reconnected with the wagon train and, hostages in tow, began the long, cold trek back to Camp Supply.

CUSTER'S RETURN WAS GREETED with the same fervor and joy accorded any victorious war party, and news of a great victory soon spread across the country. The military and the government were impressed. The public was split. Many viewed the Battle of the Washita as appreciable progress while others regarded the fight as another example of Indians being slaughtered. Contention over the correctness of what had happened would endure, but for those intent on development of the West it was a real sign that Indians could be eradicated, and momentum to that end increased.

Sheridan and Sherman both became stouter in their advocacy of full-scale combat as the key to subjugation.

Continuing public controversy only fueled the sudden and startling re-ascension of Custer's star. His name had once reached household word status and the battle against the Cheyenne cemented the Boy General in the nation's consciousness as an Indian fighter without peer. He had guided a large force through alien country in the severest weather imaginable, made a daring and forceful attack, achieved total victory, and made it back with minimal casualties.

There was, however, a nagging and unavoidable question that the military had to answer. What had happened to Major Elliot and his sixteen men? Leaving the scene without them was an action for which Custer, quite rightly, never received a reprimand.

No one entertained hope that Elliot and his improvised detachment were alive, but the bodies had to be found, and in December, Custer and Sheridan went out to have a look. They found the skeletons grouped together in a circle about four miles southeast of Black Kettle's village. Scores of arrows still sprouted through the bones of the men who had obviously been surrounded and overwhelmed by a superior force.

Though Elliot had left the scene of battle without being ordered, and despite the fact that Custer had sent out a scouting party to find him, the death of Elliot and his troops spawned division in the Seventh Cavalry that would last for many years.

No one ever assailed Custer's fighting ability. Unfailingly, he was in front when his men struck the enemy, whether it was White or Indian. The Washita conflict was no different. He had led his soldiers into the heart of the village and had fought hand-to-hand with Cheyenne warriors.

But a group of officers led by Frederick Benteen couldn't stand him personally. In whispers, asides, and occasional outbursts, Custer was branded foolhardy, vain, cocksure, and nepotistic. Even his wife was castigated. The "abandonment" of Elliot in the field served as the centerpiece for the denigration that swirled around the man the Cheyenne would forever know as Ouchess, "Creeping Panther." The dynamic of celebrity—build them up, tear them down—was a factor, as was envy.

The rift endured for many years far beyond the Little Big Horn, where Benteen's vengeful disregard for his commander played a significant role in the death of Custer and everyone riding with him.

Custer's response to the often, bold dissension is perceived by some as odd or spineless. He publicly ignored it and refused to engage his detractors. Even when Benteen's frustration boiled over into a challenge to fight, Custer meekly brushed it aside. But no cowardice existed in the offbeat general. He knew of the animosity, and he monitored it. But he never actively fought it, a reticence at once wise and practical for the man in command.

The man leading may have been vain, self-promoting, or even effete. But ultimately that mattered little. As they had in the Civil War, Custer's men knew their leader possessed the one quality all soldiers treasure most; he won. And through the Little Big Horn, nine years later, the men of the Seventh Cavalry followed him unhesitatingly into the field.

The Cheyenne lost at the Washita, but the battle was a deathblow in a single respect. The killing of Black Kettle carried a definitive message. There was no way peace could be reached with Whites. Only two options remained: surrender or fight. Large numbers of the once-free people settled onto their designated reservations.

However, just as many remained on the Plains, hunting, raiding and dying. In the end, they could do nothing more. Starving, exhausted from endless running, and possessing little other than bare hands to fight with, they dragged themselves to the place where their ancestors live today.

And today, almost a hundred forty years later, Creeping Panther is still the most prominent White man in Cheyenne folklore.

RECOMMENDED READING:

The Custer Reader edited by Paul Andrew Hutton, University of Oklahoma Press

Survivors of the Battle of the Washita. Though he received implied orders to kill everyone, Custer brought back fifty-three Southern Cheyenne women and children. Is Monahsetah in the picture? No one knows. (Courtesy Yale Collection of Western Americana, Beinecke Rare Book and Manuscript Library)

CHAPTER SEVEN

Monahsetah and Custer

1869 "MONAHSETAH" WAS WHAT HE CALLED HER and how he
chose to spell her name. She was a captive from the Washita and, though prone to resistance, had not fought against Custer and his men that morning because she was seven-
and-a-half months pregnant.

Unable to run, fight, or protect non-combatants, Monahsetah had stood outside her
lodge and watched as the Seventh Cavalry decimated her people and their community.
Her father, an influential elder named Little Rock, had in fealty to his daughter, come
to her side and was quickly shot to death by American soldiers. It was standard procedure during an attack to kill any male Indian over twelve, whether resisting or not.

Encased between columns of American soldiers, with fifty-two other women and children, she made the long, snowy ride back to the place called Camp Supply. The women prisoners were of the belief that, at some point, they would be executed. From the beginning (and all through their captivity) they had been used as sex objects by the deprived officers and men of the Seventh Cavalry. As prisoners there was little they could do but accede.

Custer's greatest detractor, Captain Frederick Benteen, described the winter at Camp Supply as one of wholesale fornication, crowned by the constant copulating of Custer and Monahsetah.

Benteen was right, and he was wrong. There was wholesale coupling, and his commander and the captive had become lovers. But what passed between them was far more complex than mere fornication.

Custer had enjoyed great appeal to women his entire life. Along with being a sophisticated, fun-loving conversationalist, there was an edgy and distinctly wild side to him that many women found provocative. His enormous celebrity as the Civil War's Boy General increased his already intense popularity with the opposite sex to a nationwide attraction.

This idolatry was a challenge to his marriage. His wife, Libbie, had grown up as a daughter of a judge and was unprepared for life in the spotlight. But she adjusted well. Her husband did too. He loved his wife, and there is no evidence that he was unfaithful to her, not until he came to the Great Plains.

The West struck a deep chord in Custer. From the onset he was enamored with everything from topography to taxidermy. He studied each subject with the verve of an ambitious college freshman, foremost the people who lived there.

Curiosity and fascination for those of a different culture coalesced into something far grander after he met Monahsetah. His short life with her tripped a mechanism that culminated in a profound revelation. It was something he hinted at often in his writings but never fully admitted, not even to himself.

Custer would always be loyal to the army. In succeeding years he took on every assignment, and in every engagement with Indians he fought to win, this despite the pronounced dualism he exuded after his time with Monahsetah. From then on, Custer not only fought

Captain Frederick Benteen of the Seventh Cavalry. His hatred of his commander was so obsessive that a quarter century after Custer's death Benteen was still railing against him in correspondence with strangers.
(Courtesy Denver Public Library)

Indians, but he also identified deeply with their way of being and especially their wild, unharnessed way of living.

Not surprisingly, what little is known of Monahsetah came from her one-time lover. In his memoirs, Custer described the extraordinary woman he knew as follows:

> Little Rock's daughter was an exceedingly comely squaw, possessing a bright, cheery face, a countenance beaming with intelligence, and a disposition more inclined to be merry than one usually finds among the Indians. She was probably rather under than over twenty years of age. Added to the bright, laughing eyes, a set of pearly teeth, and a rich complexion, her well-shaped head was crowned with a luxuriant growth of the most beautiful silken tresses, rivaling in color the blackness of the raven and extending when allowed to fall loosely over her shoulders, to below her waist.

Though some of the liaisons between other soldiers and Cheyenne women were ugly and abusive, Custer and Monahsetah's were not. Together, they would make historic inroads in the field, and it is obvious from Custer's writing that intimacy in knowledge of one another was deep.

Custer learned what her name meant in English: The Young Grass That Shoots In The Spring. He described in detail a series of pivotal events in her life before capture. He wrote that the Little Rock family was esteemed as royalty and that Monahsetah was a much sought after bridal prospect. Her father, to her dismay, arranged her marriage. Normally, two to four ponies were the going price, but a young warrior and his family offered eleven for Monahsetah.

The deal concluded, Monahsetah and her new husband set up housekeeping in his lodge, but she didn't like where she was living, her menial work, or her husband. For a time the young warrior attempted to placate his wife with congeniality and deference to her wishes. That approach proved unsatisfactory to both sides.

The tough-guy tack was then taken with results far worse than dissatisfaction. When the husband tried to assert himself with force, Monahsetah pulled a pistol from her blanket and shot him in the knee, crippling him for life.

After finding out what had happened and considering the facts, Little Rock dissolved the marriage by returning the eleven ponies.

In his final comment on the story, Custer revealed much about his new life view:

> What an improvement upon the method prescribed in the civilized world! No lawyer's fee, no publicity nor scandal; all tedious delays are avoided and the result is as nearly satisfactory to all parties as is possible.

Following its Washita success, the army was eager to pursue a regimen of pulverizing the wild tribes into submission. As usual, however, politics insisted on restraints and the policy that eventually emerged was a practically unworkable blend of war and peace.

Hostiles were to be approached with hands extended. Behind the hand of friendship would stand the men and machines of war, set to strike if the hand was not taken. Added to this delicate mix would be bands of Indians committed to defending their way of life, many of whom harbored unrequited revenge for acts of treachery by Whites.

Custer was chosen to execute this dangerous and uncertain initiative.

From the Cheyenne captives he chose three women to help accomplish the mission, a strong Cheyenne named Mahwissa; an unnamed Sioux woman; and Monahsetah.

∽∾⤬∾∾

MONAHSETAH WAS LITTLE MORE THAN A MONTH from giving birth, and the Sioux woman, though recommended by Custer for her interpretive skills, functioned primarily as a nanny before and after the child was born.

There has been testimony that Monahsetah's feelings for Creeping Panther were deep. She longed for him after they parted and was affected by his death. But emotions never dominated her feelings of obligation to and togetherness with her people. When Custer offered her the role as his translator and guide in the field she accepted it enthusiastically but imposed a condition. She told Custer she would provide the required services for as long as he wanted only if, at the end of her duties, all captives were reunited with what was left of their families and friends.

Custer agreed to the deal and kept his word, marking one of the few times in Indian/White relations a promise made by White authority was kept.

Camp Supply did not have suitable facilities for holding prisoners, and after Custer selected his three assistants, the remaining fifty captives were shipped east to Kansas's well-established Fort Hays.

As always, Custer didn't merely accept his assignment. He tackled it with a force and vigor unmatched by any man in uniform. His warrior's mentality was on a par with the most distinguished Indian braves, and he was ever ready for battle. But it was consistently clear through the winter of 1868-1869 that the man whose reputation was built on fearlessness in engaging the enemy had changed. Instead of paying lip service to the aspect of the policy that sought a bloodless subjugation of the wild tribes, Custer embraced it with passion.

He constantly led forces in and out of the field that winter, achieving unprecedented success by inducing band after band of hungry, wary, and weary people to give reservation life a try. He met ire and hostility measure for measure, taking hostages, threatening to hang some of them, and keeping his troops on the brink of attack. Custer not only succeeded in bringing in significant numbers of free roamers, he also secured the release of a few White captives, actions that lifted the spirits of everyone.

To the consternation of his soldiers, everything was done without engaging the enemy. Tramping through icy conditions on long, forced marches with skimpy rations and thin protection against the cold led his men to think of combat and victory as their reward for the ordeal.

But their commander was consumed with negotiating peaceful settlements. Few, if any other officers took the time to learn anything about language, routinely leaving that work to an often dubious and highly inconsistent corps of translators. But Custer quickly became fluent in sign language and broke through, communicating directly with elders and leading warriors, giving him extra advantage in negotiations.

Most often, Monahsetah was at his side. She had taken a few days off in mid-January to give birth but was quickly back in the saddle, trailed by the Sioux nanny and her new child. She and Custer did not always agree, but together they were formidable; their teamwork played a vital role in calming the rough waters of Indian/White antagonism.

∞⤙✕⤚∞

DEALING WITH THE DELICATE AND SHIFTING MENTALITY of the free-roamers was not the only element of challenge in Custer's precarious, high wire performance. There were many internal difficulties to overcome as well.

Throughout his career, Custer had clashed with those who supplied men in the field. At best, the suppliers of food and other provisions, known as the Quartermaster Corps, were sporadic. At their worst, they simply ignored requests or buried them deep in their well-established bureaucracy.

Then, as now, there was no accountability and Custer's contempt for lack of government support of his men was as high, if not higher, than that for enemies in battle. While putting together the Seventh Cavalry he became so infuriated at incompetence and fraud, such as sacks marked "coffee" filled with bean-like gravel, that he took the extraordinary step of jumping a train in Kansas and traveling to Washington D.C. where he personally confronted the quartermaster's top brass.

The distraction of getting supplied coincided with the widening gulf of pro- and anti-Custer divisions in the Seventh Cavalry.

Excessive drinking and alcoholism were common among officers, and sitting in their bleak, frozen camp waiting for the arrival of supplies for the field, only encouraged more.

Custer did not drink at all but looked the other way when men got drunk, so long as it was off-duty. He came down hard on people caught imbibing while in service. But he

Comanche and Kiowa assembled to receive rations at Camp Supply in Oklahoma. Government corruption guaranteed that food and material for living was routinely a fraction of what was promised. (Courtesy Yale Collection of Western Americana, Beinecke Rare Book and Manuscript Library)

did not abuse his power by punishing only those who disapproved of him. His brother, Lieutenant Tom Custer, a two-time Medal of Honor winner, was placed under arrest when his drinking got out of control.

That winter Captain Frederick Benteen's compulsive degrading of his commander reached an apex when a letter he had written to a friend in the newspaper business was published in the *St. Louis Port Dispatch*. It characterized the entire Battle of the Washita as leaderless chaos and saved its strongest prose to describe the agonies of Major Elliot and his men as they waited for help that never came.

Tom and Custer's longtime adjutant Lieutenant W. W. Cooke found the newspaper and confronted Benteen who admitted he was the author. Then they showed it to Custer himself, who responded by calling an immediate and tension-filled officers' meeting.

Overflowing with his own bile, Benteen armed himself with a handgun, hoping to provoke his boss into a confrontation. Stammering with rage, Custer demanded to know who had written the letter, and Benteen again admitted that it was he, adding a snide and juvenile challenge that asked, "What're you going to do about it?"

Faced with taking the high or low road, Custer, despite his anger, chose the former. He did nothing. Benteen seized on the refusal of his commander to fight as a stellar example of spinelessness, milking the incident as a damnation of Custer for the remainder of his life.

How Benteen could have skated through all of this is baffling. The army never punished him for publicly castigating not only his superior, but also the entire military. Custer never took action against him either, most likely because his leadership role required that he fly above petty jealousy, disdain, and other grumblings among the ranks. In a deeper, more personal sense, it was not Custer's nature to retaliate against people. Years after his death, his wife wrote that he admired Abraham Lincoln and had adopted one of the former President's remarks as a kind of mantra, "…with malice toward none, with charity toward all."

Though he would not be promoted beyond captain, Benteen stayed with the Seventh Cavalry, serving under Custer through the disaster on the Little Big Horn River seven years later.

⋙✕⋘

THROUGH THE CONSTANT DISTRACTIONS and turbulence that winter of 1869, Custer remained focused on his uncompleted mission. He couldn't stand the idleness of life in camp and constantly longed to be in the field, as evidenced in a letter to his wife:

> I shall be glad to get on the move again. I have remained in camp until I am tired of it. I seldom care to stay in one camp over two or three days. I am almost as nomadic in my proclivities as the Indians themselves.

The day after writing the letter, the twenty-eight-year-old led a force of fifteen hundred troops into the field for what would prove to be a surreal expedition. The next two weeks produced events from which the stuff of movies, plays, art, and novels are made. What might be viewed as cliché today, however, was fresh and original during those long ago two weeks in March.

This time, the new child and its nanny were left behind as Monahsetah rode next to Custer in search of the last large force of hostiles—her own people, the Southern Cheyenne. From its onset the march was incredibly grueling with a margin for error that was miniscule. After months of movement, there was no clue as to where the Cheyenne might be. The country was unknown, rations and supplies were thin, and the weather was still frigid.

Lieutenant W.W. Cooke. His loyalty to Custer was unshakeable. He was at his commander's side through many campaigns, including the Little Big Horn where he penned the last communiqué from Custer's force. After he died fighting, Cooke's enormous sideburns were scalped. (Courtesy Denver Public Library)

In four days the huge caravan covered almost eighty miles without finding much more than a trace of Indians. Food allotments had been cut twice, and hundreds of men and animals were suffering mightily from exhaustion.

Boldly, Custer cut his force in half, sending crippled men and animals back to recover and await orders. Knowing that speed was essential to any chance for success, he left the wagon train behind too and marched on into the unknown.

After nine hours in the saddle, the best his Osage scouts could come up with was a trail of fourteen horses and one lodge. Without any other leads, Custer followed the skimpy clue. Stopping only to water the horses and once to make coffee, his force rode for nineteen hours. At two a.m. they halted to sleep in the open. Screaming constantly for water, the command's horses and mules kept many men awake until reveille was sounded at four a.m.

They marched all the next day without finding drinkable water, thinking that the Indians they were following would lead them to some. This proved correct, and when, at last, they caught up with the tiny party, Custer attacked. The few Indians fled in every direction but none were killed or captured. His half-starved men replenished themselves with buffalo meat from the little encampment, but their ordeal was far from over.

Custer had been leading his men further and further from the nearest supply source, risking everything to find the Southern Cheyenne. The troops, under assault from many privations, were no longer focused on fighting Indians. As they ate up their foundering animals, focus shifted from glory and combat to survival.

When his scouts found the old marks of a single lodge and a faint trail leading away, Custer followed. The trail grew larger mile after dramatic mile until it was confirmed that they had stumbled on the scent of who they were looking for...Stone Forehead.

As Keeper of the Sacred Arrows (a Holy Grail equivalent), Stone Forehead was the highest ranking Cheyenne on the southern Plains, headman of a big village of the most hostile roamers still on the loose, estimated at more than two hundred lodges. If he and his people could be convinced to come in, the campaign would close bloodlessly.

But several nearly insurmountable obstacles impeded getting to that point. The men's adrenaline had been ignited by the prospect of battle, but most were too degraded to match the speedy pursuit required.

With a handful of scouts and a small escort Custer moved on the village as fast as possible, leaving a dangerous but necessary gulf between the main force and himself. What Custer dreaded most was panicked, all-consuming flight of the Indians. If that happened, the condition of his troops would preclude further pursuit. The only way he could avoid that was to reach them before they fled.

A further complication was the strong belief that there were White captives in Stone Forehead's village, specifically two mothers who had been abducted during the previous year's murderous raids. If the village ran, the women could not be retrieved. If it were attacked, the Cheyenne would follow the standard practice of executing their prisoners.

What Custer had to do was juggle the various elements into a configuration that would stifle the village's fear and his own soldier's bloodlust. In that fragile atmosphere there would be a small opening for negotiating the return of the White captives and capitulation to reservation life.

As they neared the village, Monahsetah confirmed that the two White women were on the premises.

A delegation of warriors appeared to find out what was going on. In a parlay with Creeping Panther, an in-village council was arranged with Stone Forehead.

It was a critical moment. The bulk of Custer's disheveled force was still approaching the village, and the Cheyenne knew they were coming. The fate of the White women was uppermost, but the entire mission was tottering between victory and defeat.

Custer's skills as a strategist and reconnoiter have been debated for more than a hundred years. But his mastery of improvisation was profound, and he now took an action so audacious and brave that it has been replicated in countless dramas ever since.

Stone Forehead's village contained several thousand people, including hundreds of dedicated warriors who had unremittingly wreaked violent havoc on Whites wherever they could be found.

Monahsetah opposed Custer's plan and, exercising her unique combination of savvy and strength, informed him that if he went ahead with his suicidal move, he would do it without her.

Custer went ahead. Trailed only by his obstinately loyal adjutant, Lieutenant Cooke, the White man called Creeping Panther rode alone into the heart of an edgy nation ready to fight for its life.

He dismounted in the center of the massive village. Cooke was hustled off and Custer was ushered into Stone Forehead's Sacred Arrows Lodge. There he sat Indian style while fifteen men, the cream of Cheyenne leadership, appeared and took their places around the fire.

Stone Forehead conducted the meeting with pronounced reverence. He pulled out a special pipe, filled it, placed it between Custer's lips, and lit it. Having smoked in council before, Custer took a few draws and started to pass the pipe to his left, but Stone Forehead's hand kept it between his lips.

Now Custer faced an additional challenge. Being a non-smoker, the more he puffed the sicker he got, and all of his grit and discipline was called upon to keep from vomiting.

While Custer turned green, Stone Forehead, famous for prophecy, sang out a series of words, repeating them until Custer had smoked his bowl. The medium's prediction is alive today, shrouded in legend. "If you act treacherous toward us, sometime you and your whole command will be killed."

At the close of preliminaries, Custer signed bluntly that he had come to receive assurances that the Cheyenne would move onto the reservation. His troops were surrounding the village and would attack if Stone Forehead and his people did not comply. He added that resistance was useless and that he would never raise a gun at a Cheyenne again if they conformed.

He was told that they would think it over, and the meeting broke up on a final fateful note. Stone Forehead emptied the pipe on Custer's boot tops, saying again that if he betrayed them he and his troops would turn to ash.

To the surprise of everyone, Custer and Cooke returned unharmed, but when he announced that the village would not be attacked his troops became disgruntled. The men wanted to fight; otherwise, what was the point of all their hardships?

Somehow Custer, who took most of the heat for inaction, managed to keep the lid closed on the bloodlust of his own men. The chronology that unfolded over the next few days was so rife with suspense, eleventh hour reprieves, and shifting scenarios that it reads like a screenplay.

∾∾⤬∾∾

STONE FOREHEAD AND FORTY WARRIORS and boys came into the soldier camp to talk. As they visited, Custer was informed that the village was taking flight. Surreptitiously, Custer moved a hundred, heavily-armed troops who were ordered not to fire, around the visitors. Then he announced that they were to be held hostage until everyone moved to the reservation. Stone Forehead and his followers broke away and rode off in a huff, but three prominent leaders were retained and disarmed. Astonishingly, no shots were fired during the chaotic jockeying.

Custer sent one of his new captive's sons off as a runner with a fresh demand that the Cheyenne return the two White women. Stone Forehead sent back a delegation offering to swap the White women for the hostages. Custer refused.

For days, a bizarre and bloodless tug of war ensued with Monahsetah playing a featured role as mediator. Various other Cheyenne leaders showed up lobbying incessantly for a swap of prisoners. Custer refused their every entreaty.

Though the village had been abandoned, its starving residents had not gone far, and Custer moved his forces closer. At the end of his rope, Custer issued an ultimatum. If the White women were not returned by a certain deadline, the hostages would be hung from a tree, and the army would hunt everyone else down.

Minutes before dusk, which would signal execution, the two White women rode into Custer's camp. Another delegation of Cheyenne ventured into Custer's camp seeking a parlay with the soldier chief. Saying they had done what he had asked, they now wanted the hostages back. Custer refused once more, reminding the Indians that they had not yet agreed to go to the reservation.

This time they agreed. They would not be able to move until they and their ponies were stronger, but they would come.

Custer marched his emaciated force east to a pre-arranged supply point. Then they moved on to Fort Hays. The hostages were still in hand, two White women had been rescued, the Cheyenne had agreed to peace, and there had been no combat casualties on either side.

∽∾⤬∾∾

IT WOULD BE YEARS before the conflict ended. Lack of food or implements to grow it would force the Cheyenne to shuttle back and forth between the reserve and their wild homeland but, at the moment, the government celebrated Custer's remarkable achievement.

Back at Fort Hays, Monahsetah did not stay in the stockade but moved freely about the installation until everything came to a head at mid-summer.

Shortly before the arrival of Custer's wife and her own repatriation, Monahsetah and her child were moved back into the stockade. Custer took Libbie into the enclosure where she was chagrined at the syrupy devotion the women rained on her and her husband. Only the older women made the fawning displays. The younger captives hung at the fringes wearing coy smiles, which Libbie regarded as suspiciously romantic.

Monahsetah was summoned from the outer reaches of the crowd. She took her time, changing out various items of apparel before she came humbly forward. Custer and his wife both held her month's old daughter, and out of nowhere Monahsetah told them they could raise her daughter if they wanted. Custer didn't respond. Libbie declined.

On the day the captives were shipped back to the West, Monahsetah walked up to Custer, raised her eyes, and left him with a knowing smile. He never saw her again, but she would see him once more.

Monahsetah did not fare well. Though she retained her dignity and remained attractive to many warriors, her actions with Custer made her something of a pariah to her own people. She moved north and in the fall gave birth to another child, a boy she named Yellow Swallow. Historians have argued over Custer's connection to Monahsetah's baby, most saying the timeline of pregnancy and birth makes Creeping Panther's fatherhood impossible. What they overlook is that their arduously researched timeline precludes fatherhood for anybody. Yet a child was born and, at the point of conception, the closest thing Monahsetah had to a husband was the Boy General.

Seven years later, on a blistering afternoon the day after the Battle of the Little Big Horn, Custer and his command were found dead and rotting on a high hill. Every soldier had been mutilated; bodies had been sliced open and faces turned to mush. Everyone with hair had been scalped.

Custer alone was intact. This was puzzling because the Sioux only knew they were fighting White soldiers. They didn't know Custer was in the fight; but even if they had it wouldn't have mattered. The Sioux did not celebrate Whites, and the women would have cut him up.

Light fell on the mystery years later when a Cheyenne woman testified that she had been on the battlefield that day and was watching a group of women pierce Custer's eardrums with awls when they were interrupted by another woman who happened on the scene. She commanded them to stop, calling the dead man they were working on a warrior.

The woman was a Southern Cheyenne who had not been long in the north. Her name was Young Grass That Shoots In The Spring... Monahsetah.

RECOMMENDED READING:
Custer and the Cheyenne by Louis Kraft, Upton and Sons

Post-war Comanche camp in the Wichita Mountains on the reservation at Fort Sill, Oklahoma
(Courtesy Yale Collection of Western Americana, Beinecke Rare Book and Manuscript Library)

CHAPTER EIGHT

Burned at the Tongue

1871

FOR GENERATIONS THE KIOWA TRIBE had teamed with their allies and friends, the Comanche, to defend and secure the borders of the enormous range they inhabited.

They had fought the Spanish threat from the south for decades before it was repelled. The wave of settlement that came to Texas from the east had, through constant raiding, been kept from penetrating the northwestern expanse constituting the Kiowa homeland.

After 1865, however, the Kiowa were occupied with battling new menaces sweeping down from the north—primarily settlers, hunters, and soldiers. It was the threat of the "long knives" that had been most difficult, forcing many Kiowa, by 1870, to accept the concept of reservation life.

With their own people split, the influx of railroads and the enormous complications they brought, the rising specter of starvation, and the weariness that comes with constant fighting, the Kiowa had little choice but to accept promises of welfare to be provided by new agents called Quakers.

For the Kiowa, like all other tribes, shifting from random roaming to reservation residence represented a classic leap from frying pan to fire. There was no food on the reservation, no way to make any kind of living, and absolutely nothing to do.

They couldn't stay, and they couldn't go; so they did both, incurring endless frustration and wrath from their agents and the soldiers lined up behind them in support of a national "peace policy." The military functioned as police, while the Quakers endured one spiritual crisis after another in their impossible roles as probation officers of the White God.

Attempts to integrate the Kiowa into a prescribed system of living were monumentally difficult. As a nation they exemplified the wildness of Indians, both in social affairs and combat. Over the generations they had been blessed with distinguished and long-lasting leadership, but the death and confusion brought by so many incursions coming at once had divided influence among many individuals.

Of these, a man named Kicking Bird was devoted to the search for peace. For years he worked to accommodate the Whites and his own people simultaneously. His efforts were of a magnitude that have given him a permanent place in history; ironically, those same efforts brought misery to his life in the form of condemnation from the opposing forces he labored so diligently to placate.

What made Kicking Bird's determination even more commendable is that his influence never extended further than over half of his people at any time, usually less.

The rest of the Kiowa followed a number of other chiefs, the most prominent three being Lone Wolf, Satank, and Satanta.

✺

LONE WOLF WAS A STOLID, PLACID-FACED MAN, unceremoniously wed to absolute freedom and willing to take on all comers.

Satank was past the age of seventy, highly respected as the senior member of an elite warrior society, and feared as a possessor of magical powers. People walked on eggs in his presence.

Satanta would have been unique in any setting. He could perform oratory with evangelical passion and splendor. He was big, bully-faced, and had earned unassailable credentials in battle. He also possessed a gift for satire that entertained not only his own people but many Whites as well. But beneath Satanta's loud, overwhelming, and often

Lone Wolf was one of the Kiowa's most effective leaders. When his son was killed by the Whites his dedication to war calcified. Even after surrendering his arms, the warrior, because of his anti-White sentiments, was shipped to prison in Florida. When he finally returned to the reservation malaria was infesting his system and he died soon after. Followers entombed him on the side of a nearby mountain, a site that remains secret to this day.

(Courtesy National Archives)

Satanta could fight and he could entertain. His oratory, especially when addressing Whites, was widely celebrated for its boldness, accuracy, and humor. For years he was jailed at Huntsville State Prison in Texas, before finally taking his own life. He, too, is buried in honor on Chief's Knoll.
(Courtesy Denver Public Library)

entertaining presence, was a perfect example of the Kiowa majority's attitude. White superiority was never accepted, leaving Satanta and those of like mind convinced that the reservation was nothing more than a weird idea that couldn't be understood and didn't work.

Satanta had agreed repeatedly to give reservation life a try, but as most other Kiowa, when the place was empty of food, he would leave to hunt and raid. To Satanta, his counterparts, and followers, there was absolutely nothing wrong with attacking and killing to ensure existence.

For their White supervisors, the Kiowa represented the largest, most unremitting headache they had ever experienced.

A Quaker named Lawrie Tatum was the Kiowa agent. In his previous life Tatum was known for intelligence, simplicity, and pure adherence to Quaker principles of faith. He remained true to his God, but Kiowa behavior couldn't be controlled, and by the end of his tenure, the mild Quaker advocated death for the chronically disobedient.

The Indians, impressed by and irritated with the agent's inability to adjust his criteria, called him Stone Head.

The military intervened on request but had been practically disarmed by the peace policy. They gritted their teeth and focused on construction and maintenance of their post at Fort Sill, Oklahoma, while conditions deteriorated.

Both Tatum and the soldiers who guarded him despised governmental behavior. Their difficult task of keeping wild people subdued on the reservation was rendered impossible by lack of support. Washington treated promises of food, equipment, and manpower as if they had never been made. For all involved, making the peace policy and the reservation system work was about the same as trying to bail water from a boat with a hole in its hull.

By May of 1870, the unworkable plan for control was nearing its death throes. The Kiowa delightfully took full advantage of the chaos. Being the height of spring, their ponies were sufficiently renewed to take the field, and, ignoring restrictions, the Kiowa went out.

Lone Wolf took his loyalists far onto the amazing region known as the Staked Plains to hunt.

Satanta, Satank, and a young fighter named Big Tree put together a war party of more than one hundred warriors and rode across the Red River to see what damage they could inflict on the long-hated Texans in the south.

Riding with them was Owl Prophet, the most respected seer among the Kiowa. It was he who had called the initial meeting that resulted in the formation of the raiders and it was he who had suggested Texas as a good target for acquiring horses and killing Whites.

In an area known as the Great Salt Prairie near Jacksboro, Texas, the Kiowa warriors took up positions on a wooded hillside above the well-traveled Butterfield stage line and waited for action. Following a spiritual consultation, Owl Prophet issued instructions that the first potential target should be allowed to pass unharmed. The second would be the right one to attack.

Owl Prophet's predictions had not always come true, but many had been inexplicably spectacular. When a wagon covered with canvas followed by fifteen mounted troops came into view, the warriors who were scattered over the hill stayed silent until the small caravan was out of view.

General William Sherman, commander-in-chief of America's armed forces, was riding in the canvas-topped wagon. Prompted by the failing peace policy, he was on an inspection tour visiting various army facilities up and down the Plains.

Sherman did not like the West and was weary of the nation's wavering over what to do about the "Indian Problem." It was his belief that force should be applied without letup to make the Indians surrender. While waiting for the light to change he had made frequent journeys West where he found nothing to like about the country or its inhabitants. The naiveté of the settlers was perplexing, and the Indians were little more than wild creatures who must be caged.

On his many trips to the frontier he had seen little in the way of Indian depredation and regarded reports of such as hysterical exaggeration.

Owl Prophet's mystically-shaped strategy not only saved the general's life, it shifted history. Had Sherman been killed and scalped that May afternoon, the nation's majority would have lobbied loudly for decisive action, action that would have brought unrest on the southern Plains to a speedy and gory conclusion.

Little more than an hour after Sherman went unwittingly on his way, a second group of White travelers came into view. A dozen teamsters were manning ten wagons filled with corn purchased by the army. The train was being pulled by more than forty mules, a valuable find for the Kiowa.

Years earlier Satanta had been gifted with a military bugle at a treaty meeting. He carried it constantly and had learned to blow charges and retreats that sounded like the real thing. The frustrated warriors jumped the gun, however, charging down on the doomed wagon train before he could press the instrument to his lips.

The drivers tried in vain to move their cumbersome wagons into a circle. Several were killed on the first Kiowa pass. The remainder made for the cover of a wood line, but two more died as they ran.

The attackers' preoccupation with the train and its livestock saved five of the teamsters who, though injured, somehow escaped death that afternoon.

The Kiowa suffered three dead, one of them having his face shot off as a wounded driver popped up from the bed of a wagon. The driver was quickly disarmed, bound face-down on a wagon tongue, and mutilated while a fire made on the ground below

As a warrior no Kiowa was more revered than Satank. A ferocious fighter, still formidable in combat at age seventy, he also possessed deeply mystical qualities and a short temper. The sash across his chest was worn only by the ten bravest warriors in the entire Kiowa nation of which he was one. He was shot and killed in an attack on soldiers transporting him to trial and lies buried in a place of honor atop Chief's Knoll at Fort Sill, Oklahoma. (Courtesy Denver Public Library)

burned him up from head to toe.

All but one of the drivers, who was bald, were scalped, the mules were gathered, and the war party, flush with success, started back north.

After interviewing one of the survivors the next morning, Sherman quickly ordered a unit of troops into the field to give chase. But a storm front dropped inches of rain, that washed out the Kiowa tracks, and the pursuit was dropped.

Continuing his tour, Sherman stopped at the attack site during a makeshift memorial for the seven dead drivers and addressed grieving families and friends. He told the Texans that the outrage would not be tolerated, giving them his personal guarantee that the leaders of the atrocity would be apprehended and punished. This sentiment quickly spread through military posts in the area, putting everyone on the lookout for the general's culprits.

The wait for revelation did not last long. Two weeks later the Kiowa came in for allotment day at Fort Sill. Lawrie Tatum's headquarters were there as well, and he called the Kiowa leaders to his office for a meeting. There he asked Satanta, Satank, Big Tree, and several others if they knew anything about a recent attack on a wagon train in the south.

Without hesitating, Satanta spoke up. After upbraiding Stone Head Tatum for the government's failure to provide promised support, he admitted to having led the wagon train raid, going so far as to say that if anyone else claimed leadership they were lying.

Tatum instantly fired a communiqué to the neighboring military authority, demanding that Satanta and the other principals be arrested without delay.

In General Sherman's presence Satanta, Satank, and Big Tree were taken into custody. Satanta argued that several warriors had been killed in the attack and that he figured they were even. Sherman countered that attacking twelve men with a hundred warriors was cowardly, and if Satanta resisted arrest he would be shot to death.

After a flurry of legal and military maneuvers, two wagons were requisitioned, along with an escort of soldiers, to carry the three prominent warriors to the frontier hub town of Jacksboro where they would stand trial for first-degree murder.

With hands and feet shackled, the three indicted men were loaded into the wagons. Satanta and Big Tree were in one; Satank was alone in the other.

As soon as the wagons were underway, Satank pulled a blanket over his head and began singing his personal death song. Unbeknownst to the soldiers in the wagon and those riding alongside, the old, tough warrior gnawed at one of his wrists as he sang, finally tearing away enough flesh with his teeth to free both hands. Tossing off his blanket, Satank pulled out a secreted knife and stabbed the soldier nearest him. As he tried to ready a rifle, the old warrior was shot multiple times. His body was dumped at the side of the road where it lay overnight. Relatives retrieved it the next day.

Satanta and Big Tree arrived safely in Jacksboro where, in a packed courtroom, they were judged by a jury of settlers, all of whom had lost family, friends, or acquaintances to Indian attacks in the past.

Though the outcome was never in question, the warriors' assigned lawyer, a man named Woolfolk, didn't behave as though the cause was lost. Instead, he attacked the proceedings with heartfelt passion. Woolfolk claimed the court had no jurisdiction in the case and that the jury was biased against the defendants. Woolfolk was correct on both counts, but his objections were denied.

He then demanded that the defendants be tried separately because of their disparity in age (Satanta was over fifty, Big Tree barely past twenty).

This request was granted as was a last, far more important one. If the Kiowa men were found guilty and sentenced to death, Woolfolk insisted that the judge promise to draft a letter to the state's governor, seeking clemency. He described his clients as "intelligent human beings" and told the judge that unless he acceded to this last demand, Woolfolk would remove himself from the case.

Aware that any delays would jeopardize the already tense proceedings, the judge agreed to solicit the governor and provide a two-month window between sentencing and execution.

Big Tree was tried first and quickly convicted. When an interpreter asked if he wanted to speak before sentencing the young warrior declined.

Satanta's conviction came with the same speed, but unlike his comrade, the skilled speaker seized the opportunity to make a proclamation before the judge ordered him to be hung by the neck until he was "dead, dead, dead."

He addressed the Texans crowding the courtroom directly, expressing condolences for all the fighting and vowing never to take up arms against them again if he were allowed to return to his people. Satanta testified that he had sought friendship with Whites since he was a child and concluded his extemporaneous speech with a warning than rang of truth "… if you kill me," he said, "it will be like a spark on the prairie. It will make a big fire. A terrible fire."

After he sat down, the judge ordered him hung on the same day as Big Tree at "some convenient place near the courthouse."

∞⤬∞

BUT AS THE WHEELS OF JUSTICE SPUN FORWARD, Satanta's prediction was coming true. Knowing that Satank was dead and beset by rumors that Satanta and Big Tree had been executed before they reached Jacksboro, most of the Kiowa fled the reservation.

Lawrie Tatum, already beleaguered by inexplicable headaches and dizziness, was on the verge of seeing all the modest gains he had made in converting the Kiowa vanish. His Quaker friends were writing in large numbers, suggesting that by soliciting Satanta and Big Tree's arrest he had helped sentence them to death, a decidedly un-Quaker-like action. Representatives from the Texas legal system pressured Stone Head Tatum into committing a clear crime by tampering with crucial evidence. In his original letter to the military requesting the Kiowa arrests, Tatum had omitted Big Tree's name.

When the Quaker told the Texans that he was certain Big Tree was on the raid, too, they insisted that this truth needed to be in the evidence. Tatum redrafted the letter, inserted the name Big Tree, signed it, and gave the paper to the Texans for use in court as an original document.

Old Stone Head would remain the Kiowa agent for nearly two more years, but the wildness of the Indians, the duplicity of his own government, sporadic cooperation from his military protectors, and ongoing pressure from his brethren in faith would make his tenure schizophrenic on all fronts.

The judge in Jacksboro fulfilled his pledge and wrote a letter to the governor of Texas. Cleverly worded, the missive impersonally advocated clemency and the governor, whose publicly stated intention as a leader was to erase Texas's many blemishes, bought the rationality of the idea.

A month before they were to hang, Big Tree and Satanta had their sentences commuted to life imprisonment at Huntsville State Prison in eastern Texas.

The incarceration of the two important warriors provoked a serious change in the Kiowa. The people loved Satanta in particular and were desperate to have him back. He was not just a warrior, diplomat, and orator. He was a true celebrity among them and the Whites as well. Compared to the wildness of the recent past, the Kiowa settled down. Conflicts and violent clashes continued but not nearly as often as before.

While the Kiowa waited, the prisoners passed their days in the company of White rejects. Big Tree was described as a quiet, hard-working man who paid stoic attention to the ways of the Whites.

Satanta, in a rare description rendered by a reporter from the East, maintained his dignity as he passively resisted the standard of being just another prisoner:

> I saw a tall, finely-formed man with bronzed complexion and long, flowing brown hair—a man princely in carriage on whom even prison garb seemed elegant...Satanta had come into the work-room...where he never performed a stroke of work...(he) had seated himself on a pile of oakum, his hands folded across his massive chest.

Big Tree was thoughtful, dutiful and, as a young man, spectacular in battle. After serving a prison term he returned to the reservation and eventually converted to Christianity, living out his life as an elder in the Baptist church and repeatedly expressing sincere regret for the violence of his youth.
(Courtesy Denver Public Library)

When informed that the reporter wanted to conduct an interview, Satanta "motioned me to be seated with as much dignity and grace as though he were a monarch receiving an ambassador...he hardly seemed over forty, so erect, elastic, vigorous was he."

Lobbying for the release of Satanta and Big Tree went on unabated, but the longer they stayed in prison, the less compliant their people became.

Conditions on the reservation continued to get worse. Young men became harder to restrain and going beyond the bounds of their assigned territory, whether by straying or raiding, resulted in violent confrontation with soldiers, settlers, and Texas militia-men.

It soon became clear that there was leverage to be had by using the two leaders in prison. The federal government began to pressure the Texas governor for a release of the convicts in hope of calming down the Kiowa once again.

Despite the adamant objections of Stone Head Tatum, General Sherman, and his own constituents, the governor agreed to free the Indian chiefs. In return the Kiowa on the reservation promised to take the White man's road, and two-and-a-half years after they had been put behind bars, Satanta and Big Tree were reunited with their overjoyed people. Satanta, far less effusive now, gave up the red arrow marking him as a war leader and resigned his chieftainship.

The peace was short-lived.

∞✕∾

IT WAS 1873 and White hunters by the hundreds were illegally flooding onto Indian ground in the rush to slaughter huge, southern herds of buffalo.

Raiding picked up once more, but now the consequences were greater. Attrition was closing on the Kiowa. More and more leaders were dying on the prairie, but worst of all, their promising sons—the future of the nation—were dying just as rapidly.

Satanta brought his followers in and, accused of violating the conditions of his parole, was returned to prison without a trial.

His reprieve was over, and there would be no more freedom for the chief who had completely earned the adulation his tribal members bestowed on him.

Several years passed and, as they did, Satanta grew appreciably older and more despondent. He pined most of all to be with his people again.

In October of 1878, he was standing in a second floor infirmary awaiting medication when longing overpowered a traditional Kiowa taboo. The great Satanta flew through an open window and ended his life.

Seventy years later he did return to his people when his body was exhumed and re-interred at Fort Sill on what is called Chief's Knoll. There, not far from the famous, well-preserved fort, a hillock graveyard rises at the edge of a modern, sprawling army installation. Uniform headstones of army dead surround the rise.

On top lay the Indians, mostly Kiowa and Comanche. Lying there together, they represent the closest equivalent of an Arlington National Cemetery that American Indians have. Along with Satanta, the remains of many people are situated atop the hill, including Quanah Parker, Kicking Bird, and Satank.

The narrow escape of General Sherman and the killing of seven drivers hauling corn had started a morbid process that obliterated a nation.

For the Kiowa there is no more fitting epitaph than the words of one of their own. Satank, considered by Whites to be old, nasty, and irascible, had spoken to them at a treaty conference. Thankfully, someone took the trouble to record what he said:

We have warred against the White man but never because it gave us pleasure. Before the day of oppression came, no White man came to our villages and went away hungry. It gave us more joy to share with him than it gave him to partake in our hospitality.

In the far distant past there was no suspicion among us. The world seemed large enough for the Red and White man; the broad Plains seem now to contract, and the White man grows jealous of his Red brother. He once came to trade; he now comes to fight. He now covers his face with the cloud of jealousy and anger and tells us to be gone, as the offended master speaks to his dog. We once gave you our hearts. You have them now.

Kicking Bird (actually Striking Eagle) was a strong Kiowa warrior and a forward thinker. Early on he perceived the futility of warring against Whites. For years he tried to be a bridge between the Whites and his people. The futility of the task was equaled only by Kicking Bird's courage and determination. When everyone was locked down on the reservation resentment flared. A powerful medicine man named Owl Prophet threatened Kicking Bird with death and several days later, after drinking his morning coffee, the valiant warrior became violently ill and died from what was later ascribed to strychnine poisoning. (Courtesy National Archives)

RECOMMENDED READING:

Kiowa Years by Alice Marriot, University of Oklahoma Press

CHAPTER NINE

The Palo Duro

1874 A MODERATE NUMBER OF TEXAS RESIDENTS know the place called Palo Duro Canyon. Each summer a musical extravaganza extolling the virtues of the state is staged on the northern floor of the canyon. Thousands come to see it, but few who have visited the place are aware of its full enormity, and fewer yet have any inkling that a way of life was put to death within its confines.

That loss affects every set of feet in America today. But it would take countless queries before any person could be found who recognized the words "Palo Duro."

It is the second largest canyon in the United States and ranks high on the planet's long list of spectacular formations. Often plunging to depths of one thousand feet, the canyon cuts finger-like across the Texas Panhandle for more than a hundred miles. A river runs through its heart, supporting life in multitudes. The Palo Duro is more a geographic region than a canyon, and almost every American lives and dies without knowing it exists.

The canyon lives on, but the depth of meaning it held for the lords of the southern Plains is lost.

The Comanche and their allies were the last descendents of more than ten thousand years of human life to reside there. What the Comanche lost was not just the Palo Duro but a gigantic land mass the size of Texas itself that they had rigorously overseen for two centuries.

Palo Duro Canyon (Courtesy Tom Bean)

This vital part of the empire they controlled, the Palo Duro, provided a haven for as many Indians as wanted to winter there. The buffalo came down too, and there man and beast passed generations; they were safe from the wrath of blizzards on the Plains above and utterly untouchable to the enemies on their borders.

When the great culture of the Comanche, Kiowa, Cheyenne, and other tribes died, it did so in the typical ironic fashion of history. Everything came to an end in the one place that had always been invincible. The Palo Duro.

The final demise began with a coming together. The Medicine Lodge Treaty had essentially stated that if the southern Plains tribes remained peaceful and stayed put, the U.S. government would guarantee that White encroachment on their territories would not be tolerated. Though all bands had not signed the agreement, and despite the American government's shameful history of not honoring its promises, the treaty worked until American entrepreneurs found something to exploit south of the Red River, in Indian Territory.

Having cleared the entire state of Kansas and much of Nebraska, the leaders of a new and insatiable industry wondered if there was not more product to be found on the Staked Plains of Texas. Everyone was clamoring for more—shippers and processors, middle-men, and especially rich consumers in the East who slavered over the melt-in-your-mouth buffalo tongues that filled a whole platter and made an "all you can eat" meal. The tongues were a rich delicacy for the many who could afford them.

Buffalo coats were heavy but profoundly effective against the cold; the floors of well-appointed homes, when graced with the thick, luxurious hides from beasts in the West, were walked on with pride.

Millions of the buffalo were killed in the early years of the 1870s, but by 1874 demand was rapidly exceeding supply. The hunters had killed everything they could find, and now the prairies were coated with billions of whitening bones. But south of the Red River large herds were thought to exist. The work of killing, skinning, and transporting was hard and ugly, but the money was too good to pass up. Treaties, government policies, and even the threat of scalping and mutilation at the hands of outraged warriors could not stop the lure of commerce. Business surmounted all other concerns. Encouraged by burgeoning corporate interest, the countless bands of uncouth slaughterers crossed illegally into the south.

The invasion of Whites and the destruction they wrought with their big guns would shortly spark the fire of full-scale warfare, but the foundation had been laid long before unscrupulous hunters came into the country.

For years the government had tried to inveigle the Comanche, Kiowa, Cheyenne, and Arapahoe to settle into reservation life, but the results had been badly mixed. The ques-

Despite making millions for ranchers, the cow never fared well on the Great Plains, being acutely vulnerable to common and radical changes in climate. The Buffalo was and is perfectly suited to existence there, and as a food source, its meat is vastly superior to beef in nutritional value to the human body. The gigantic pile above represents a tiny fraction of bones from the scores of millions who were slaughtered to the edge of extinction. Near the end of the nineteenth century their remains were still being gathered off the land for processing into fertilizer. (Courtesy Detroit Public Library)

tion over whether or not to take the White man's road had already shattered the inherent unity of tribes, bands, and families.

The factions that had given it a try had put themselves in the unenviable position of go-betweens. Men like Kicking Bird, a Kiowa whose efforts toward peace were tireless, tried valiantly to accommodate both White and Indian. But under the circumstances his efforts and those of many others were in vain.

It was the same for the upstanding members of the Quaker religion who, early in the decade, had brought an intriguing proposal to the president of the United States. The "Indian Problem" in the West had long been a divisive public issue for which there seemed no solution. But the sentient Quakers had conceived an idea that might put an end to the frustration. Honest and caring members of their faith were ready, willing, and able to assume the role of agents for the wild tribes. Not only would the Indians be treated fairly by scrupulous agents, they would also be indoctrinated into the wondrous fulfillment of devotion to the White man's God.

Innovative and naïve as the plan was, it was supported totally by the president. Anything would be better than the currently dysfunctional state of the reservation system, and politically there was no way to lose. Indian haters and lovers alike would have a hard time quarreling with pure men of God taking over the care and guidance of unruly savages.

Mission-driven Quakers fanned out all over the country, including the huge Comanche/Kiowa reservation on the southern Plains, to right wrongs and pave the way for peace. Their well-intentioned work would never reach its hoped-for heights. In fact, it never got off the ground.

〰️➳✖️➲〰️

HOW TO ESTABLISH AND MAINTAIN a structured life on the reservation was a puzzle they could not solve. Many Quaker agents were frustrated beyond their imaginations with the indecision, the changing of minds, and the overall unpredictability of Indian behavior. When the reservation had something to offer they came in. When it didn't, they went out. The chaos of this was constant.

Despite their grinding annoyance at the ephemeral quality of their wards, all the Quakers understood, to different degrees, that there was justification for duplicity among the Indians. The government the Quakers represented betrayed them on every level.

Roving bands, who were persuaded to come in on the pledge that the "Great Father" would take good care of them, routinely waited weeks for overdue beef rations, during which time it was easy for many to fall prey to the distraction of whiskey, a substance that shocked their brains into insanity.

When beef did appear it was never in good condition; it was always lame, sick, or underweight. And quantity was invariably less than expected. Rations earmarked to last the reservation a month were often gone in days.

The Quakers split their time between entreating the government and assuring the Indians that help was on the way. It never came, and though many Indian/Quaker friendships were built, the agents would eventually lose all credibility in the eyes of their clients. And vice versa.

In addition to bald, rampant corruption and an unending string of broken promises, Indians on the reservation found themselves suddenly vulnerable to criminals. Gangs of White Texas horse thieves descended frequently on the inert reservation residents, stealing Indian ponies whenever there was an opportunity. The same White gangs took their strategies to higher levels in the field. There they continued the wholesale thievery of horses and attacked freight wagons, often murdering drivers and escorts while disguised as Plains Indian warriors. Eventually, they were found out, but the unwanted complication of White marauders only spun the situation further out of control.

This morass of confusion exploded into disaster with the coming of the buffalo killers. No Indian could envision a sacred animal being gone from the earth. But it wasn't long, however, before the native people understood that the buffalo would disappear if action was not taken. Even those who were convinced that opposing the White wave was futile could make no argument against an effort to stop the massacre, and many peace-promoters joined what was the greatest unification of tribes ever seen on the southern Plains.

Hoping to exterminate the exterminators, the Indian army of nearly a thousand warriors swept north across the Panhandle toward a place called Adobe Walls. It was there the financiers of the slaughter had brazenly established a settlement in Indian Territory, complete with a hotel, saloon, and various other structures that served as a hunter's headquarters while the great southern herds were decimated.

Rumors of Indians on the move and sheer coincidence had brought about thirty productive hunters to Adobe Walls on the eve of the attack.

Focused on the retail town as the spot where they could do the most damage, the Indian legions approached their target with care, knowing that surprise was crucial.

Unfortunately for the defenders of the buffalo, the vagaries of fate were against them. A pair of brothers who had funded Adobe Walls and were making massive amounts of money from the annihilation happened to be in the area. Through pure chance they and their manager discovered that the rumors about Indians descending on Adobe Walls were true.

Exercising the corporate mentality that places the dollar above all else, they instructed the manager at Adobe Walls not to tell the assembled hunters of the impending attack, lest they flee and leave the facility open to destruction.

In the darkness of early morning on the day of the assault, the manager fired a pistol and woke the hunters, most of whom were asleep in the hotel. He told them that a critical section of roof was breaking and must be repaired immediately. Thus the hunters were awake and quick to respond when the river of outraged warriors borne on the thunder of thousands of hooves surged in from the east.

Outnumbered by more than thirty-to-one, the hunters were perfectly positioned and perfectly armed to repel the attack. The warriors tried to penetrate the buildings housing the enemy for hours, gallantly performing feats of pure bravery. In desperation, some attackers went so far as to claw barehanded at doors and walls.

But they failed. The fortifications were too strong, and the massive rifles inside, their shells blowing huge holes in the bodies of the warriors and their ponies, were too big.

By mid-afternoon the huge, Comanche-led force had withdrawn to a ridgeline near-ly a mile away. Various leaders were discussing options when a stray bullet fired from Adobe Walls struck a prominent medicine man's pony in the forehead, killing the ani-mal instantly. Taken as proof of White invincibility, the random shot effectively ended the battle of Adobe Walls and marked the beginning of a much larger war that would change the character of the southern Plains forever.

Three Whites were killed at Adobe Walls, but scores of irreplaceable warriors were no more. Many others were horribly wounded. In grief, disillusionment, and anger, the huge war party broke into smaller groups and set out to spend the summer terrorizing Whites in every region of the country.

The wholesale outbreak brought the national peace policy to an end. Quaker agents resigned or were relieved en masse and the military, which had been sitting grumpily on the sidelines for almost five years, was brought to the fore.

≈≈✕≈≈

IN THE COMING MONTHS, anarchy ruled the plains of Oklahoma and Texas. While organizing strategies, the military pursued a sideline of keeping those committed to reservation life in place while enticing intractable elements to give themselves up. Nothing worked.

Divisions inside the tribes became systemic. Those running free despised those who had surrendered, and those who had surrendered were pressured from all sides to flee. Depredations and open combat continued unabated through the summer, but by September the United States Army was set to activate a massive movement to kill and subdue the hostiles once and for all. Finally, the convictions of those contemptuous of the gutless peace policy were given free rein.

Five huge expeditions would march onto Indian Territory from five directions, each of them led by seasoned, high-ranking commanders eager to carry out the government's about-face for war.

The column marching up from the south boasted six hundred soldiers, including the renowned Fourth Cavalry. Augmenting the force was a large supply train of wagons and twenty-five Indian scouts, among them a dozen Tonkawa, the hated, cannibalistic ene-mies of the Comanche and Kiowa.

Each troop, scout, and freighter in the column was under the authority of a man the president had called "the most promising young officer in the army." He was also one of the strangest. Colonel Ranald MacKenzie's body still carried shrapnel and bullets from his distinguished service during the Civil War. He had been advised by doctors to quell his incessant pain by taking opium, but MacKenzie rejected medications in favor of keeping a clear head for duty. He showed little interest in personal advancement, the opposite sex, or glory in any form. He was alternately described as eccentric, aloof, unpredictable, ill tempered, and overbearing.

Like his contemporary George Custer, however, he was nothing less than a great fighter and had deftly adjusted to the many nuances required in battling Indians. In the previous, rudderless years he had clashed with the Comanche numerous times, and after being humiliated and out-foxed, he was entering the field with the benefit of hard lessons learned well.

Having lost two fingers in the War Between the States, he was known to the people of the southern Plains as "Bad Hand."

The pressure of the five columns was immediate. Suddenly, White soldiers were coming from everywhere, and the pursued resisted with all the power they could muster. Supply trains were attacked and soldiers were harassed whenever possible. Much effort was made in throwing the army's tentacles off track, and some of the columns found themselves stalled for want of provisions or new directives.

Ranald MacKenzie didn't stall. For all his oddities, MacKenzie's character could be defined with one word: relentless.

He knew when and how to deploy in uncharted country while chasing warriors whose skill in combat was profound. He knew when the distance between his soldiers and their provisions was acceptable and when it wasn't. He knew when a large band of warriors broke away from a trail of hundreds, that it was a ruse.

He didn't make camp the night the warriors made their desperate diversion. Instead, he force-marched his men deep into the morning when his scouts rushed in with news of an astounding discovery. A canyon of unbelievable size was just ahead.

He made the rim before first light, and when there was enough dawn to see the canyon floor, he realized that what at first looked like hundreds of strange growths were actually tipis bunched for miles along a band of water winding through the great canyon.

A trail, so narrow that men would have to lead their horses down, was located, and MacKenzie made a decision. Surprise was always a crucial factor in war, but in these circumstances, it meant the difference between victory and defeat. If the enemy found his troops sneaking slowly along the cliff wall, the result would be horrific.

He sent them down as soon as the stomach-churning trail was found. Near the bottom, a Kiowa sentry was waiting. When he saw who was coming, he fired his rifle and ran off waving a blanket.

One of America's greatest warriors, Ranald MacKenzie's prowess on battlefields was equaled by his oddity of character. While still in uniform, his mind shut down and the military committed him to an insane asylum. On his release the outstanding Civil War and Indian fighter took residence with his sister where he died before reaching fifty.
(Courtesy National Archives)

In another environment warriors hearing a shot at dawn would have been out of their beds and onto their ponies in seconds. But on this September morning fate tilted toward the Whites and turned its back on the Indians.

The Kiowa who had seen the soldiers on the cliff face hurried to his lodge and began to apply warpaint instead of rousing anyone.

Many bands were camped too far up the river to hear the shot. Those who did were exhausted from running and, never having seen Palo Duro penetrated, figured it never would be. They went back to sleep.

By the time the sun sneaked over the canyon's edge, Bad Hand's force had made it down to the floor and was charging up the river.

Considering the number of people involved, the battle was practically free of blood and gore. The fighting lasted most of the morning, but the warriors, encumbered with moving women, children, and the elderly to safety, battled the White men with one hand. Only three were killed.

Not one of MacKenzie's men died that day. Their commander was everywhere, constantly shouting out orders and providing first-hand guidance. MacKenzie regarded getting the Indian's possessions as vital to victory; he wanted their homes, food, clothing, and weapons. More than anything he wanted their ponies. A free-roaming native without a pony was as impotent as a vehicle without wheels.

Deploying a company of troops to capture the horse herd, MacKenzie was gratified when they returned from a two-mile foray up the canyon pushing an enormous number of animals, almost fifteen hundred, in front of them.

Safe on the high rims, hundreds, perhaps thousands, of Indians watched as MacKenzie's troops reduced everything they owned to ash. Winter was already pressing in, and they were left with what presently covered their bodies and nothing to eat. Late in the afternoon, they saw their ponies driven up and out of the canyon and many from the Palo Duro had no choice but to go into their respective agencies and lay down their arms.

Eight months later the amazing Comanche, Quanah Parker, led four hundred people—the last of the free—into Fort Sill, Oklahoma and gave up forever.

Parker's surrender, however, was not much more than a piece of punctuation, marking the end. The end had come at the Palo Duro or, more precisely, about twenty-five miles south of the battle site.

There, after more than thirty straight hours in the saddle without food, MacKenzie ordered a halt to give rest to the troops and see to unfinished business.

Twice before in his career the Indians had recaptured ponies taken from them and Bad Hand was not going to let that happen again. Three hundred of the best animals were distributed as bonuses to officers and scouts.

The remainder, more than twelve hundred animals, were executed by MacKenzie's infantry. For years afterward many of the troops who pulled the triggers were haunted during their waking hours and disrupted in sleep by bad dreams.

The bones of the dead Comanche ponies lay in high piles for many years before being gathered up by cash-hungry farmers who carted them off to be sold as fertilizer.

The last to surrender, Quanah Parker was a Comanche with a rare heritage. His mother was a famous White captive. Following capitulation he quickly ascended to high leadership, was embraced by Whites, and became the most effective chief in reservation history. Throughout, Quanah Parker remained a traditional Comanche, maintaining multiple wives. Seeing a near-fatal lack of morale in his people he introduced peyote on the reservation as a spiritual aid. Today, despite constant government pressure to cease, peyote ceremonies are widespread throughout the United States. (Courtesy Yale Collection of Western Americana, Beinecke Rare Book and Manuscript Library)

Today, at the place where so many died, fragments of their once free-running bones can still be found all over the ground, the last vestiges of the Lords of the southern Plains and the lives they led.

RECOMMENDED READING:
The Buffalo War by James L. Haley, State House Press

Not far below Last Stand Hill is a panoramic view of the Little Big Horn Battlefield. In the distance, beyond the treeline, thousands of tipis stood. The pathway at the left marks the on-going retreat of Custer's command. Higher up, the Boy General and about fifty of his men fought to their deaths. (Courtesy Drex Brooks)

CHAPTER TEN

The Greasy Grass

1876

COMPARED TO THE LIKES OF WATERLOO, the campaigns of Alexander the Great, Gettysburg, or the Crusades, it is a small event.

But in the annals of battle it exceeds all others in controversy, mystery, and enduring public fascination. Human minds all over the globe recognize the primary participants.

The fight lasted only a few hours, but it was far more than a collision between armed adversaries. It was a culmination of hostility between Indian and White, a final showdown between cultures that, ironically, turned the effect of winning and losing upside down.

Indians called it The Greasy Grass, but worldwide it is known as The Battle of the Little Big Horn.

The Deadly Plan

BY THE CLOSE OF THE YEAR 1875, tribes on the southern Plains had been decimated to the point that compliance with the government's plan to incarcerate what was
left of the Kiowa, Comanche, Cheyenne, and Arapaho on reservations was complete.
The buffalo were gone, warriors were dead or disarmed, and remnants of once great
nations were under the full control of Whites.

Relations with still wild tribes, the largest and most dominant being the formidable
Sioux Nation, were in full disarray.

Former war leaders such as Red Cloud and Spotted Tail had decided they had no
choice but to give in and had been long engaged in a cold war with White authority in a
hit and miss attempt to make reservation residence survivable.

But thousands of Sioux, led by men like Crazy Horse and Sitting Bull, were still free
and did not consider any other life. To them, the idea of living on a reservation was as
far-fetched as changing the color of their skin.

For years politics had dictated that responsibility for addressing the "Indian
Problem" be passed to and fro between the president, various branches of the government, and the army, a constant inconsistency that rendered federal dealings with wild
tribes on par with a shell game.

In the fall of 1875 the bureaucracy of the Commissioner of Indian Affairs had been
placed in charge, and a new initiative, based on capitalism, was being promoted. A series
of meetings between representatives of Indian Affairs and the Sioux, in which America
offered to buy out established Indian Territory (especially the potentially rich Black
Hills) had been held. The Sioux responded by placing an astronomical price on their
holdings, and the commission threw up its hands.

After consulting with other agencies, high echelons of the military prominent among
them, a devious plan was hatched. In November of 1875 the Indian commissioner issued
an ultimatum: all free roaming bands of Sioux were to report to the reservation by
January 31, 1876. Those who did not come in would be considered hostile and subject to
punishment by the army.

Runners were sent out with the directive, but many remote communities were never
reached. Those who were shook their heads. Even had they wanted to, the Lakota people
could not have responded. The northern Plains were frozen, ponies were weak, and having families and the elderly trek hundreds of miles through such conditions was suicidal.

Lack of accord with the ultimatum was what the United States had hoped for, and a
massive, winter campaign against the Sioux was already in place when the deadline passed.

The plan had been formulated by leading military minds and, from its inception, was made inept by arrogance and ignorance. The same type of scheme had been used at the Palo Duro two years before with brutal success; but this one turned out far different.

The ultimatum issued by Indian Affairs was nothing more than a license for genocide, and every involved government official knew it. But getting the insidious scheme from paper to reality was a process fraught from the start with hindrances that would transform the advantageous proposition of a winter campaign to that of a dangerous foray conducted at the height of summer.

The primary supply line for the northern Plains was the massive Missouri River, usually a reliable and, compared to travel over land, speedy thoroughfare. But the winter of 1876 was deathly cold and the river froze.

By the first week of February 1876, General Philip Sheridan, who was in charge of the American Army's field operations and a mastermind of the deadly plan, had everything in place. The favored hunting grounds of the recalcitrant Sioux would be descended on by overwhelming columns coming from three directions.

General George Crook would lead fifteen hundred soldiers from the south. From the east, General Alfred Terry would come with a full cavalry regiment and several companies of supporting infantry. Commanding the Seventh Cavalry was Sheridan's strongest fighter and long-time quasi-protégée, George Custer. Coming in from the west would be nine companies of cavalry and infantry led by Civil War veteran Colonel John Gibbon.

Sheridan was desperate to pull the trigger on a conclusive winter assault, but he could not. The weather made it impossible for Terry's or Gibbon's forces to take the field. Crook's huge command was the only one with a chance to do damage, and Sheridan sent him out.

Crook's first engagement against a northern Cheyenne village, in mid-March, was so botched by a sub-commander that the venerable, Indian-fighting Crook withdrew entirely, opting to wait until spring before going out again.

By April the wide Missouri was finally breaking up, the snows had ended, and the three columns were at last supplied and ready to go. But on the verge of raising flags another obstacle suddenly jumped into view. The seven hundred fifty men of the Seventh Cavalry had no commander. He had been subpoenaed East to give testimony before a Congressional committee investigating fraud in the Department of War. Custer's absence delayed the plan to attack the Sioux for another critical month.

But the delay took a back seat to the external and internal crises Custer created for the army. What Custer said at the hearing brought near-total devastation to his career and came within a whisker of saving his life.

CUSTER COULD HAVE AVOIDED the subpoena on perfectly legitimate grounds, but he answered it arbitrarily because it pushed a long-festering button in his dutiful psyche. Corruption in the War Department's Quartermaster Division had infuriated Custer through all his years of service. Nothing piqued his ire more than seeing his troops receive foods that were years old, enduring endless short cuts on allotments, and being subjected to outright theft. For years, he had railed publicly against the criminal behavior of his suppliers and, not long before, while stationed at his current post, North Dakota's Fort Abraham Lincoln, he had placed the entire neighboring town of Bismarck under arrest when tons of military supplies were found cached in private hands.

When the secretary of war (soon to resign under threat of impeachment) visited Custer, his wife Elizabeth, knowing the depths of her husband's disgust, applied all her energies to keeping the two men apart to insure that Custer's rare wrath would not boil over into an ugly, possibly physical confrontation.

Though he was a lifelong Democrat, Custer's political allegiances were varied. The committee chairman was a minority Democrat, a Republican (Ulysses Grant) occupied the White House, and both parties were engaged in an ongoing political war. The Boy General stepped into the middle of it all.

For two days Custer spilled all he knew, implicating the secretary of war and the president's brother in a conspiracy to hand out military contracts to shady suppliers in exchange for lucrative kickbacks. What Custer told was the truth, but it gave him instant persona-non-grata status in the country's highest political and military circles. Ironically, Custer's testimony, though it generated a wave of negative publicity for the Republican administration, was judged hearsay and never entered into the Congressional record.

Whatever flaws Custer possessed, the most profound among them, especially in view of his public stature, was a colossal and immovable naiveté. From boyhood his unique nature pushed him far from the mainstream. He was never aware of the subtleties in political and economic operations. Like the Indians he fought much of his life, Custer saw only the face value of what came his way.

The one vendetta Custer ever pursued was government corruption, and it brought his naked naiveté into the open where it was summarily pulverized.

The general of the army, William Sherman, suggested (ordered) Custer to pay his respects to the president before he left town. Early the next morning, the Boy General handed his card to the president's secretary and took a seat in the White House's reception room. He sat through the hours leading to lunchtime and continued his vigil into the hours of midday. Something was definitely amiss, but on he waited. Late that after-

Custer and his wife stand surrounded by intimates in front of their home at Fort Abraham Lincoln. Devoted to the arts, they often staged skits or held concerts inside for a constant stream of visitors from the east. It was here that Elizabeth Custer first learned that her skilled husband, who had no peers for zeal and strength in combat, was dead.
(Courtesy National Archives)

noon, already humiliated by so many hours of expectation, he was casually informed the president had retired for the day.

Leaving a note asking pardon for any offence, Custer immediately sought out Sherman. It would have been important to confide what had happened at the White House and, anyway, protocol dictated that all officers pay respects to their top commander before leaving the city.

Sherman wasn't there.

Twice that evening Custer appeared at Sherman's residence in a city hotel. The general was absent, and no one knew where he was.

In a maelstrom of confusion, doubt, indecision, and fear, Custer boarded a train for

Chicago, there to make a connection with a line that would carry him back to his assigned frontier post and his loyal wife.

On arrival in the Windy City he was met by one of General Sheridan's key aides and several troops. A telegram had been received from General Sherman that said of Custer:

> ...he was not justified in leaving without seeing the President and myself. Please intercept him and await further orders; meanwhile let the expedition proceed without him.

Custer had been relieved of command and, though unshackled, was under arrest.

In a panic he threw together a telegram to Sherman, explaining in detail his efforts to comply with what was required. Sherman's response didn't address what had taken place but directed him to travel to St. Paul, Minnesota, the headquarters of his immediate superior General Terry.

Shortly after his arrival another telegram came from Sherman. He had just seen President Grant and the nation's top executive had decreed that Custer could return to Fort Abraham Lincoln and resume his duties but that he was not to accompany the expedition.

Reduced to tears, Custer begged General Terry for advice and was told his best chance at redemption was a direct appeal to the president. Under Terry's editorial eye, Custer drafted a brief and poignant entreaty. "I appeal to you as a soldier to spare me the humiliation of seeing my regiment march to meet the enemy and I not to share its dangers."

The desperate telegram alone could not have changed Grant's mind. He had known Custer for years and had never liked him. The damage the recent political embarrassment the Boy General's whistle blowing had caused was not repairable, and Grant was determined to professionally castrate the out-of-step leader of the Seventh Cavalry.

But Custer's telegram was not the only request Grant received. Behind the scenes Sherman, Sheridan, and other planners of the all-out war on the Sioux brought pressure on the commander-in-chief. Without Custer, the mammoth campaign would lack its most consistently determined fighter. In short, the campaign's successful outcome was predicated largely on Custer's proven tenacity and leadership in combat.

The army won out. Grant relented via Sherman who telegrammed Terry saying that if he wanted Custer to go it was now alright to do so. In his final communiqué, Sherman advised that Custer refrain from taking any newspaper reporters with him and to cast no more aspersions but rather adhere strictly to business.

Custer did not follow the former instruction (the reporter that came was killed at the Little Big Horn), but he executed the latter unfailingly.

The Seventh's commander returned with just enough time to organize the regiment for action. It was a hectic and exhilarating two weeks. Custer would be leading a large force that included a big portion of his family. His brother Tom would be leading a company of the Seventh, as would his brother-in-law, James Calhoun. Another brother, Boston, was retained as a forage master, and Custer's nephew "Autie" Reed had signed on as a herder.

Through the flurry of activity leading up to departure there was but one insistently negative note, which emanated from Custer's wife. Whether from the paranoia that must have ensued from the aftermath of the visit to Washington or from purely prophetic vision, Elizabeth Custer had been plagued by nightmares portraying her husband's death and mutilation. After a barrage of pleas from his wife, Custer finally sat down and had his hair trimmed short for the first time in years.

The haircut might have alleviated some of Elizabeth's fears, but she remained distraught. When the column of more than twelve hundred moved out on May 17, 1876, she did not wave as the large force passed by. She went with them and camped one last night with her husband before going back to the fort.

As they rode along on their last day together, the wife of the army's most famous soldier was spiritually felled by a final, striking portent. A rare, atmospheric oddity known as a sun dog suddenly appeared. Through a mysterious configuration of temperature, light, wind, and other elements the entire column was suddenly and definitively reflected in the sky overhead; this was a chilling sign that the Seventh Cavalry was marching into heaven.

Custer did his best to calm his wife's raw nerves, telling her that he had experienced exactly the same phenomenon on his way to victory at the Battle of the Washita. But the next day, at parting, she was still on the verge of breaking down when she finally faded from view for the last time.

Custer marched west. These were the moments he lived for, moments free of bureaucracy and politics and boredom. He was leading men into combat.

But the campaign had missed its start by months, and the feisty ponies of the Sioux and their allies were growing stronger by the day.

Bright and dedicated, Lieutenant James Calhoun was married to Custer's sister. He was one of five members of the Custer family who died at the Little Big Horn. (Courtesy Denver Public Library)

One Hundred Pieces of Flesh

THE SIOUX AND THE CHEYENNE WERE NEVER DUPED by the ultimatum issued at the end of 1875. They knew exactly what the Whites were up to and, through years of experience, knew that a climax was coming in their lives. The U.S.'s obvious intent to conquer was confirmed by the abortive attack on the Northern Cheyenne village in March of 1876.

The problem of Indian people was the same it had always been; what could possibly be done to stop what appeared to be unstoppable?

Anxiety was present in lodges all winter, but when spring finally began to break, a course of action that would relieve the weight of stress and worry was devised by one of the world's greatest leaders, the Hunkpapa chief known as Sitting Bull.

By 1876 he was too old to be an active fighter, but his reputation among the Sioux, based on his incredible record as a warrior, had been cemented years before.

Now he was a spiritual leader without peer. His astuteness in worldly matters was impeccable and the implacable expression reflected in his photographs is an accurate mirror of his dedication to the holy life way of the Sioux.

Sitting Bull had seen the divisive and debilitating effect years of reservation life had on his people. He had seen every agreement between Indian and White broken. Now huge numbers of soldiers would be coming onto the Plains to fight.

Sitting Bull knew too that his people were weary of fighting, alarmed by the rapid disappearance of the buffalo, and perplexed by an uncertain future. Instead of accentuating the negative, however, Sitting Bull that spring issued a wholly different call. It was a cry that resounded across the northern Plains. Its appeal went to the depths of every Indian soul, even those on the reservations. It asked the Sioux and Cheyenne to gather on the Plains one more time to hunt the buffalo and be together in honor of the way of life they all loved.

The response was astounding. Every branch of the expansive Sioux Nation answered the call, as did the Cheyenne. Singly, and in groups, people living on reservations drifted out to the prairie. Two months later the greatest assembly of Indian people ever seen on the Great Plains had been established next to the Little Big Horn River.

At least a thousand lodges hugged the winding waterway at intervals extending more than a mile. The pony herd was estimated at twenty thousand.

It was as if all that was sacred and divine had been restored to its rightful place of prominence. Spirits ran higher than could have been imagined, and each member of the enormous congregation was quickly infused with feelings of invincibility. If the "Long Knives" were to come, now it would be at their own risk.

Sitting Bull.

Gilbert

Mandan, Dak.

Though he did not fight at the Little Big Horn, Sitting Bull was the most prominent architect of victory there
(Courtesy Yale Collection of Western Americana, Beinecke Rare Book and Manuscript Library)

The strength of spirit was lifted higher by the actions of Sitting Bull himself. On the night before a sacred Sundance was to commence, the elder Sioux made a sacrifice that impressed the thousands of fellow tribesmen and Cheyenne encamped with him.

Sitting Bull wanted to receive a vision from the dancing to come, and in preparation, he demonstrated his commitment to that end. Sitting straight up, he instructed his adopted son to remove one hundred pieces of flesh from his arms (fifty from each). Using a sharp-bladed knife, the boy, in a lengthy operation, cut away the small pieces of his father's skin. At the end of the mutilation Sitting Bull's arms were running red. He stayed seated long into the night, until the blood had coagulated.

The next morning he began to dance. He took no breaks for food or water and stared open-eyed at the sun for hours. His body collapsed at midday and, as men came to his aid, Sitting Bull announced that his vision had come. A voice had spoken to him and, in Sitting Bull's own recollection, it said:

> I give you these because they have no ears.
> I looked up and saw soldiers and some Indians (enemy scouts) on horseback coming down like grasshoppers, with their heads down and their hats falling off. They were falling right into our camp.

The vision's content was immediately announced and soon spread through the gigantic camp. Any White soldiers venturing in would be defeated. The Sioux and Cheyenne could not be conquered. The already rampaging sense of power and security reached greater heights.

Several days later the spiritual attitude was tested when outlying scouts brought word that a large force of soldiers was on the march.

It was Crook's column, thirteen hundred strong, led by an additional three hundred hated Crow and Shoshone scouts, coming up fast from the south.

The multitudes camped along the Little Big Horn went straight to action. Widely regarded as god-like in battle, Crazy Horse announced his intention to repel the soldiers, and warriors came to him by the hundreds. That night Crazy Horse led a thousand fighters through lightless and rugged terrain for thirty miles.

After riding all night they attacked early the next morning.

The force and the size of the assault threw Crook's command into disarray; what is known now as the Battle of the Rosebud was fought all day in chaos.

The troops maintained three shaky and shifting fronts, and several times Crazy Horse and his fighters came close to making penetrations that would have resulted in a rout.

Despite the resolve and valor of Crook's soldiers, a breech would likely have been made were it not for the Crow and Shoshone. Often engaged in hand-to-hand combat that day, the Crow prevented several near breakthroughs, and when the Sioux finally withdrew, it was Crook's Indians who had saved the men in uniform.

Though he would always characterize the fight as a victory, Crook also withdrew from the battlefield. Each side had its losses, and a significant number of soldiers were suffering from wounds. He marched his column south and settled into camp.

The real reason for Crook's withdrawal was that his force had been badly shaken. They had fought a confused battle against powerful fighters that had come close to inflicting far greater damage on them. For the next few weeks Crook and his army hugged a pleasant stream called Duck Creek and licked their wounds, both physical and mental.

Years later one of Crazy Horse's followers at the Battle of the Rosebud casually stated the simple reason for the Sioux withdrawal that day. They were "tired and hungry."

Those who had died were mourned with unabashed grief, the traditional Indian response to death. Wailing and self-mutilation ran up and down the avenues of the great village, but Crazy Horse's success in blunting the White offensive raised confidence to the level of celebration.

Custer was coming soon, but to the phenomenal gathering along the banks of the Little Big Horn, he constituted no more threat than could be found in a weather change or the sudden appearance of mosquitoes.

Come On Big Village Be Quick Bring Packs

TERRY'S COLUMN (with Custer in charge of the Seventh Cavalry) paused several days' march from what would become the Battle of the Little Big Horn to confer, make final preparations for combat, and send out large scouting parties to locate the approximate position of the enemy.

Custer, Terry, Gibbon, and other officers talked things over for several days. No one had heard from Crook, and final plans were made for two columns instead of three. Lack of tactical concern over the absence of one third of the campaign force reflected the chronic over-confidence the army had in engaging Indians.

The revised plan called for adjustments in the two remaining columns. Terry would join Gibbon coming from the north while Custer, alone with the Seventh Cavalry, would ride a prescribed route to the west and swing up from the south. Together they would pin the Sioux. Terry's predominant worry, shared by everyone, was that the Indians would escape.

On June 17, Custer's second-in-command, Major Marcus Reno, returned to report on his extended scout. He had located an extraordinarily large trail leading west. Reno had found it by deviating from the orders he had been given and was soundly chastised. The action was typical of Custer's second-in-command. He had served with distinction in the Civil War, but by nature he was secretive, confused, and unstable, traits that would foment terrible consequences in a few days.

Terry instructed Custer to follow the discovered trail and issued written orders that have been analyzed incessantly ever since; some believe they were followed, and some believe they were disobeyed.

Despite a total lack of communication, Terry had the idea that both columns would descend on the enemy simultaneously, a concept that was little more than a pipe dream. Terry did understand the nuances that called for improvisation in the field and expressed in writing "that Custer should attack the savages wherever found and as to the manner of the attack, of course, was left to the discretions and judgment of Custer."

Everyone on the campaign shared Terry's unexpressed feelings. Who wouldn't want their best fighting unit to strike the enemy first?

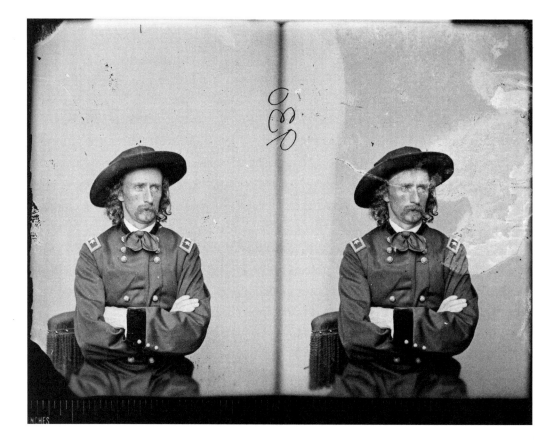

RIGHT: *General Alfred Terry commanded America's Little Big Horn campaign in the field. A former lawyer, known for a sentient, non-combative attitude, his written orders to Custer have remained in conjecture for one hundred thirty years. But the conclusion is quite clear: At a critical moment Terry unleashed his fastest, most aggressive hound and encouraged him to go get 'em.*
(Courtesy National Archives)

OPPOSITE: *In the Civil War Custer earned a fantastic reputation. At age twenty-four he commanded the Union Army's Third Division of Cavalry, a force of ten thousand horsemen. Always in front on a charge, Custer had eleven horses shot from under him while receiving only one minor wound during the war.*
(Courtesy National Archives)

Accompanied by dozens of Crow and Arickaree scouts, the Seventh Cavalry started west along the Rosebud River.

It was an eerie trip. Most had never been in the country before, and the landscape was unsettlingly queer. The light was odd. The trail they were following was growing so large that it was theorized that the route was layered with previous passages.

Custer was behaving strangely. He was his usual self in his acute hunting mentality but had changed in meetings with his officers. Normally terse and dominant, Custer on the Rosebud was open and easy in conversation with his subordinates.

Adding to the strange environment, their commander's jolting personality shift was disarming. After a meeting in which Custer's newly-gentle behavior was on full display, two officers were talking when one blurted out the subconscious feelings running through the regiment, "Are we marching to Valhalla?"

There was no answer.

Custer was thinking about the campaign, the whereabouts of the enemy, and the aspects of duty. Bubbling alongside the responsibilities of command were thoughts of redemption. The trauma of being brought to his knees by superiors was more devastating than his conviction in court-martial years before. Now he was hopelessly humiliated and looked foremost to his strengths for salvation. Finding and defeating the enemy was his life's forte, and in the few days before and throughout the battle itself, he applied himself obsessively to accomplishing his mission.

Many twists of fate would work against them all at the Little Big Horn, but neither deviation from orders, cravings for glory, nor strategic blunders played roles. No one could have imagined that they would be facing fighters whose numbers were significantly larger than their own, fighters who would be defending their race and its reinvigorated spirit.

∞⧳∞

ON JUNE 25, 1876, the defeat that numbed America with disbelief and horror was choreographed not by a single moment of dissolution or incompetence but a long series of fateful turns that brought victory to the Sioux and Cheyenne.

Custer on the march. His trusted scout, Bloody Knife, kneels at his right. The dogs sprawled on the ground were but two of the normal contingent of a dozen or more Custer brought into the field. On cold nights he would usher the whole entourage into his quarters. Several would be crammed with him on a small bed. It was no secret that many humans did not match the regard he held for dogs and horses.
(Courtesy Little Bighorn Battlefield National Monument)

Strangeness of the terrain and the weird calm of Custer were soon joined by concern over Crook and his large column. No one had heard or seen anything to indicate their whereabouts or condition.

If they had known of Crook's defeat and withdrawal, the approach to the Little Big Horn would have been radically altered. But Custer and his men never knew.

The Seventh Cavalry rode on, dragging a growing pile of doubt behind it.

Thirty-six hours before the battle, events and the urgency that came with them began to accelerate.

Custer's Indian scouts and their White commanders had been in the field day and night, following every path that sprang up, hoping to get a concrete idea of the enemy's location and size. The main trail they were following was continuing to expand, but as yet there was no precise confirmation as to where the Sioux and Cheyenne might be.

With the trail getting hotter, Custer ordered a forced, all-night march. The move was designed to put his men in position to attack should the opportunity present itself. This move has been routinely critiqued through the years by those who fault Custer for wearing out troops and horses prior to combat. In fact, expending tremendous energy to get in place to attack was routine, and when it came time to fight the men of the Seventh Cavalry, many of them veterans, went into battle fueled by the power of adrenalin.

While the troops rode silently through a night so dark that hands could not be seen in front of faces, the scouts forged ahead. A few hours past midnight they reached an observation point called the Crow's Nest, which at dawn afforded a long-distance view of the Little Big Horn Valley.

The eagle-eyed Indians in the Crow's Nest reported the existence of an enormous pony herd. Smoke from cooking fires, even at a distance of twenty-five miles, indicated a village of similar proportion. But the White scouts could see nothing.

Custer was sent for. He too could identify nothing but an empty, limitless landscape. One of the scouts looked Custer in the eye and told him there were more warriors in the valley than he had ever seen before, but Custer still wanted harder evidence before committing his troops.

So many have condemned Custer for venturing recklessly into battle, but the still-young commander held back, hoping for better intelligence. For a time he considered sequestering his troops for the day before engaging the village, this despite reports from scouts that they had been seen by wandering parties of Sioux and Cheyenne.

Not long after coming down from the Crow's Nest, however, there was a change in plans. A pair of soldiers who received orders to backtrack in order to retrieve items lost during the overnight march reported that the enemy had been found on the back trail pawing through the lost items and, on being seen, had fled.

The revelation brought Custer's and the army's greatest fear to the front. If the Indians got on the run the campaign might fail. There was enough in rations and forage to last the column little more than a week, and it was likely that what was left would be exhausted in a chase with doubtful conclusions. Months of tribulation and planning might be lost.

At the same time Custer was receiving information that the combatants, long thought to be no more than a thousand, could now be two or three times as many. That Custer would attack a force of that size has been questioned throughout history with the conclusion often being that lust for glory was his motive.

It was true that Custer paid numbers little mind. There was a sole common denominator that connected attacks on Indian villages, no matter the size. Warriors always fought under the disadvantage of retreat. Women, children, and the old and infirm were the top priority, and warriors saw it as their duty to provide a buffer as huge contingents of non-combatant families fled the fight.

In years of venturing onto the Plains this had been Custer's own experience as well. He and the rest of the army shared but one, all-consuming concern. Would the enemy get away?

When they were only a few miles from the great encampment, Custer halted and routinely divided his force, a common tactic that had produced previous victories for him and other commanders.

The cavalry was separated into three battalions. One would be led by Major Reno, a doubtful officer whose sentiments lay with the anti-Custer faction inside the Seventh. The second battalion was to be commanded by Captain Frederick Benteen, a long-time, unabashed Custer detractor. The two officers could have been sidestepped, but in the same way he had been loyal to General Terry's instructions for the march, Custer adhered reverently to the army's seniority system in selecting Reno and Benteen. The Boy General would command the third and largest battalion.

One non-commissioned officer and six enlisted men were selected from each company to serve as reserves while protecting the wagon train bringing up the rear, effectively removing slackers and the inexperienced. In all, roughly five hundred mounted troops would take the field against the Sioux.

Benteen's battalion was sent west, then north, to scour the country. Should they engage the enemy the hostiles were to be pushed northeast toward the village.

The two remaining units moved upriver from the south for a few miles before they parted. Custer instructed Reno to ford the Little Big Horn and attack the village from the south while he led his force north along a high sloping ridge, traveling parallel to the village across the river. At a point yet to be determined, his own battalion would attack from the east.

Reno led his detachment across the river, formed for battle as soon as the village came into view, and sounded the call to charge.

Two cavalrymen couldn't stop their horses and were carried to certain death inside the village. The rest of Reno's men (about one hundred twenty-five) never made it that far. The surprising volume of return fire forced them to pull up, dismount, and form a skirmish line in the open.

Some of Custer's force could hear and see the fighting. All the troops had been informed prior to battle that it would likely be the fight of their lives, and the resistance to Reno's charge was the first confirmation that it would be.

The Sioux and Cheyenne were surprised by the sudden appearance of Custer and his men, but they didn't care. Fresh from victory and emboldened by numbers, they were ready to fight.

Reno's skirmish line held for a short time. The body of warriors in front of them was swelling and, as they grew, they advanced. When it was clear that if they stayed they would be overwhelmed, Reno swung his force back like a door against the heavy growth of trees and bushes lining the river. A second stand was made here, but it was no more effective than the first.

Major Marcus Reno requested a federal hearing several years after the Little Big Horn but the revealing procedure only muddled his name and reputation more. He was finally discharged from the army after he was caught peeping at night into the post commander's home, his eyes on one of the officer's young daughters.
(Courtesy Denver Public Library)

As they emptied their rifles as fast as possible, all could see that the enemy was swarming. They were not only pressing the front, they were infiltrating the growth the soldiers were using for cover.

Everything began to fall apart. Major Reno had grown so apprehensive that he mounted his horse, and then suddenly dismounted.

A man named Bloody Knife (Custer's most trusted Indian scout) was standing next to the now indecisive major when a slug from a Sioux rifle struck his head in just the right spot and exploded his skull. Bloody Knife's brains sprayed onto Reno's face and body.

Jumping back onto his horse, Reno started to run for the river. Whether he actually gave orders to retreat will never be known, but regardless, there was nothing organized about it. Every man ran for himself and his life. Some never even knew there was a retreat and ended up cowering in the thick trees for a night and a day.

The race to the river was full of death. Many never made it across the water. Those that did found themselves scrambling up exhaustingly steep earthen slopes to a depression on top of the ridge where they set up a redoubt.

Reno survived the retreat along with little more than half the men he had gone into battle with, and given their position, it wouldn't be long before they would all die. They were in the open, and the depression could be fired upon by the higher, hilly elevations that surrounded it. The Sioux and Cheyenne easily trapped the survivors and would have overwhelmed them had it not been for the attraction of a more exciting fight that was developing a few miles north.

While Reno was still engaged, Custer's battalion continued north. The village was an awe-inspiring sight, but it did not frighten the Seventh Cavalry's commander. Rather it ignited the fighting mechanisms lodged in his brain.

The column had traveled only a couple of miles when they reached a long, wide ravine called Medicine Tail Coulee that fed straight into the Little Big Horn. The breadth of the ravine made it practical for attacking the heart of the big village.

Though the encampment's size had not struck fear it instantly altered the set up. A sergeant was dispatched to race back to the pack train with instructions to bring ammunition immediately. As the sergeant rode off, Tom Custer yelled that he should find Benteen's battalion and tell them to come on.

Ten minutes later the Seventh's bugler was ordered to ride back, find Benteen, grab up more ammunition, and come on. Because the Italian bugler's English was poor, Lieutenant Cooke scribbled hastily in a pocket notebook.

The note still exists, and its exact words are: "Benteen Come on Big Village Be Quick Bring Packs W. W. Cooke Bring pacs."

The bugler rode off. His was the final glance at Custer and the more than two hundred men of his immediate command. Barely an hour later all would be dead.

About five miles back the sergeant found Benteen and his troops watering their horses for the second time in two miles. He relayed Tom's verbal message and rode excitedly among the men saying the enemy had been found. Then he continued on to find the pack train.

Benteen and his men could hear firing along the river ahead. They moved toward it without urgency.

A mile later Custer's bugler found them and, saying they should hurry, handed Benteen the message. Benteen read the note, pocketed it and, true to a vile nature, used his first words to criticize the battle document for not being dated. He then had a discussion with his officers concerning the note itself. Were they to come right away, bring the pack train, or what? Benteen finally led his battalion forward but not at a high rate of speed.

At an inquiry years later Benteen testified that he was convinced that Custer and his

THE GREASY GRASS 137

men were dead at the time the bugler delivered Cooke's message, a brazen lie designed to exonerate himself. Dead commander's orders are defunct and cannot be disobeyed.

Benteen arrived at the depression holding Reno and several score of survivors in time to save them but far too late to spare Custer and his men from annihilation.

Reno was a mess—liquor-breathed, bug-eyed, and confused. The enemy was firing from all angles. One of the battalion's surgeons was already dead, and the wounded were sitting ducks. Horses were going down everywhere. Ostensibly, Benteen took command and managed, through experience and grit, to keep them from being overrun and slaughtered.

Fewer than three miles north, Custer's battalion, the nation's most elite group of fighters, was on the verge of a horrifying disintegration.

They knew nothing of Crook's defeat, or Sitting Bull's vision, or the overwhelming spirit they were about to face.

A detachment was sent down Medicine Tail Coulee to ford the river and attack but it was repelled with a ferocity that alarmed the command. At that moment thoughts of victory were supplanted by those of survival.

Indians poured onto the battlefield. A large party under the leadership of a Hunkpapa Sioux named Gall charged into the withdrawing troops, a strike that sent deep shivers through everyone.

Units were hastily deployed in a practical manner, but the enemy was surging in from everywhere and none could hold.

Custer and fewer than fifty others were the last to die, making their stand at a high point on the ridgeline. Warriors in the hundreds had surrounded them, raising so much dust that in the battle's finale visibility was poor and sporadic.

The coup de grace came with the arrival of Crazy Horse. He and his followers swept in from behind the surviving soldiers and swept over them. Within minutes the last man was dead.

Bodies of Whites were scattered all over the western face of the ridge, on the crest of the east side, in ravines, and along the river. The expanse where the dead fell led early analysts to believe that a panicked rout had taken place, but today the best estimators expose a mostly calculated defense by the Seventh Cavalry, a conclusion long supported by Indian testimony.

For many years eyewitnesses, who were fearful of retribution, kept mum. When, at last, they began to speak there were accounts of insane pleas for mercy and last minute suicides. But the great majority of the Indians who fought that day described the Seventh Cavalry as organized and willing to die fighting.

Nowhere was this more evident than on the site at the high point on the ridge, universally known as the place of Custer's Last Stand.

The dead horses and soldiers were found in a crowded cluster of carcasses. By that

641.   Gall.   Leader at the Custer Massacre.
The Great Orator of the Sioux Nation.

Gall led the first, devastating assault on Custer's command, a blow that spun the unit into disarray from which it never recovered. On returning to the village, he discovered that several members of his immediate family had been killed in Reno's attack. He lived for many years after the battle and his staunch, powerful aura was often captured on camera. (Courtesy Yale Collection of Western Americana, Beinecke Rare Book and Manuscript Library) time the bodies were swollen and blackened by summer heat. Identification was made more difficult by massive mutilation and disfigurement. Feet, arms, and legs had been amputated. Bodies had been decapitated and butchered.

Like everyone else Custer was stripped, his only apparel being a sock on one foot. But compared to his brother Tom, who could only be identified by a set of initials tattooed on a forearm, Custer was unscathed. Awls had been driven into his eardrums and several witnesses saw an arrow shoved into his member, but compared to the others he was pristine.

Two neat bullet holes, one in the temple and one on the side of his chest, were the obvious causes of death, but, according to those who saw him, the Boy General didn't look dead at all. Everyone agreed that he looked like he was asleep.

The Seventh's commander was propped in a near-sitting position against the similarly naked bodies of several other soldiers, his rump against the ground. His face was resting casually against the hand of an arm crooked at the elbow.

Most intriguing was his expression. All the faces of the dead that could be read reflected the terror of violent death, all but Custer's. There was no grimace of pain, no fear or anxiety. Those who saw the dead man's face were fascinated by the peace and contentment his last expression projected.

The Sioux and Cheyenne had already run before Gibbon's column arrived two days after the disastrous fight. Reno, Benteen, and their survivors and wounded were freed from the depression they had huddled in for two days, and the newly-arrived soldiers addressed the ugly and wrenching task of sequestering hundreds of their dead brethren.

No one had shovels or other tools for digging, and most bodies were blanketed with skimpy coverings of dirt and shrubbery. The officers, including Custer and his brother Tom, were scantily buried in graves only inches deep.

Gibbon and his people constructed a plethora of wooden stakes to mark the fallen and then departed, escorting survivors on the long march to safety.

Colonel John Gibbons' column, driving down from the north, was somehow expected to attack the Sioux simultaneously with Custer's force. Instead they arrived two days later, the lead scouts finding what at first sight was thought to be a ridge covered with dead livestock. (Courtesy Library of Congress)

An early map of the battlefield sketched from the accounts of Indian eye witnesses and survivors. Like all other drawings and photographs, it cannot compare with a live visit to the site. For the well-informed or the merely curious, the experience is strikingly the same, especially on days when few are present. Walking the Little Big Horn brings speculative sight into mind; soldiers scrambling up bluffs, waves of warriors sweeping over hillsides, clusters of brave men sharing the last moments of life. Everything is vivid. (Courtesy Yale Collection of Western Americana, Beinecke Rare Book and Manuscript Library)

For a full year the bodies of those who had died were unattended. When the army at last sent an expedition to gather remains and tidy the battlefield for its place in history, the bones of the dead and their horses had been scattered by various scavengers. Remnants of the common soldiers were interred in a number of locations, and the massive piles of horse bones were buried close to the marker that towers over Last Stand Knoll today.

Custer's skimpy grave was located and exhumed. A skull and a section of vertebrae thought to be his were recovered, but the remaining fragments were only enough to fill the bowl of a hat.

These bits and pieces of the man whose fame still lives were shipped to the military academy at West Point where they were placed in the cemetery. A tall obelisk marks the spot.

Next to the monument lies another grave, that of Elizabeth Custer. She survived her husband by fifty-seven years, never remarried, and devoted most of her energy to defending and pre-empting widespread attacks on a husband whose performance at the Little Big Horn has been vilified ever since.

That the couple resides together in death satiates the ideal that a precious union has been preserved. But that is not accurate. Elizabeth is there but Custer is not.

Most of his body is part of the earth on the faraway battleground in Montana. But more important, the heart and soul of his existence lies there too.

Like the men he battled and could not resist identifying with, Custer's life expired in the fashion dreamed of by all warriors. He died facing the enemy, and like his Indian counterparts, it was for Custer a route to the hereafter paved with high esteem.

For the two men of the Sioux whose leadership defined greatness, however, the road to the Milky Way and beyond would have little to recommend it. Unjust and undeserved, the ends of Crazy Horse and Sitting Bull provide a sad reflection of the final fate of America's free-living people.

RECOMMENDED READING:
Vanishing Victory by Bruce R. Liddic, Upton and Sons

Soldiers posing in front of an Indian lodge at Camp (later Fort) Robinson, a warehouse for processing incoming Sioux and the site of Crazy Horse's assassination (Courtesy Nebraska State Historical Society)

CHAPTER ELEVEN

You Have Hurt Me Enough

1877 HE WAS BORN INTO A FAMILY that was neither rich nor poor, a family that was humble but respected despite having little influence in warfare. His father was a village holy man who selflessly doled out spiritual support to anyone in need.

His mother was dead, but in traditional Sioux fashion his father remarried quickly, providing his three children with the solid maternal element necessary for growth and development.

Known to all as Curly in his early years, the casual moniker said little about what he would become but spoke volumes about what he was. The Sioux did not possess curly hair, but his was wavy and light in color, as was his skin, a pronounced oddity among Indians. He was so different that American emigrants who saw him at an early age often wondered if he was a White captive.

The man we know as Crazy Horse rose to prominence in a way that people today can hardly imagine. Wealth played no role in his life. Politics and the inherent manipulation that comes with it was not a factor either. He was a being rather than a personality, a being that is still revered by those who are convinced of the mystical power he possessed. So unique was he that his own people called him The Strange Man.

He prepared to fight by taking meticulous care in everything from his own clothing to his horse's painting, to consultations with selected elders. No matter how the fight might be going the wild shouts of "Crazy Horse is coming" spiked the adrenalin of every warrior on the battlefield. In war, the words Crazy Horse were synonymous with victory.

Death was common among aspiring warriors, but Crazy Horse, who showed remarkable courage and skill through every step to warriorhood, survived every battle in which he fought, a feat that added enormous weight to his public standing and leadership in combat.

In the eyes of his people the success he produced was linked to the dream he received on the vision quest (a prerequisite for warriorhood) he had taken as a teenager. In essence, the epiphany revealed him on a dancing warhorse. The horse was painted in a distinct design, as was his own body. From that time on he would be unfailing in following what he regarded as the vision's instructions.

The overall message of the vision was not only illuminating but also profoundly prophetic. It clearly foretold that the enemy would never be able to wound or kill him. The only real threat could come from behind, from his own people.

As Crazy Horse shot toward the legendary status he is so rightly accorded today, several seminal events occurred.

His name had been upgraded from Curly to His Horse Looking, but during a series of spectacular war performances it changed again. His father, in a gesture of respect, took the name Worm for himself, and gave his former name to his son. The boy once called Curly became Crazy Horse.

❧

THERE WERE SIX SIOUX NATIONS containing thousands of warriors, and each had the right to name a single individual as a "shirt wearer"; the ultimate warrior.

The Oglala branch chose Crazy Horse.

In his early teens he had witnessed first-hand the duplicity of the Whites (he was present at the reprehensible Grattan fight) and had since considered them the enemy. But not just another enemy. White culture repulsed him. He never attended treaty meetings with government officials, never traded, never took captives, never allowed his picture to be taken. The further he and his followers stayed from anything White, the better they felt.

In adulthood, Crazy Horse's strangeness was as glittering as his dominance of death in battle. He had a close-knit handful of longtime friends but he spoke little. When he did talk it was predominantly to children. He attended few councils, and the lack of family gave him free time, the majority of which he spent alone in the hills, isolated in meditation. In war he killed the enemy but had no interest in the traditions of taking scalps or postulating about his achievements.

He worshipped nature, in particular the overwhelming thunder, which he considered the Creator's voice. For all his abnormalities and his lofty position there was no meanness in Crazy Horse, and he was most content when minding his own business.

He may have been a mystical Lord to a vast number of Sioux, but there were many who were jealous and resentful of his celebrity. When an ugly incident occurred, one that tainted his life before death, the minority of Crazy Horse degraders scored a blow against him.

⊷⊶✕⊷⊶

DURING HIS LATE TEENS, Crazy Horse had fallen completely for a girl who came to be known as Black Buffalo Woman. Heartbreakingly, her family arranged a marriage with the parents of an already established warrior, No Water.

At age thirty, Crazy Horse was still a bachelor, status that added greatly to the queerness with which he was viewed. In retrospect it appears clear that he had remained unmarried because of an inability to overcome his powerful love for Black Buffalo Woman.

Shortly after the death in battle of a close, life-long friend, Crazy Horse and Black Buffalo Woman eloped consensually. As a shirt-wearer his primary responsibility was to scrupulously defend the welfare of his people, and taking another man's wife, while technically legal, was a precarious action. Black Buffalo Woman was within her rights to leave a situation she did not like, and traditionally, the abandoned husband would swallow his humiliation and make no fuss.

No Water didn't. First-hand testimony about the warrior characterizes him as an ambitious, thug-like man. Ignoring the likelihood that he would become a laughing stock, No Water pursued the lovers in a rage.

When No Water found them, he shot Crazy Horse in the face at close-range, grabbed his wife, and fled. At first, word spread that Crazy Horse was dead, but miraculously, the slug that had torn across his face was not fatal. Aside from the vicious scar he would carry for the remainder of his life, Crazy Horse made a full recovery.

A venerable and efficient commander, General George Crook was thought of by Indians as firm but fair. In his pursuit of fairness, Crook often clashed with higher powers in government but remained a "company man" dedicated to achieving positive results. He always regarded Crazy Horse's incredible influence as a dangerous threat to stability and considered the warrior's removal essential to implementation of policy.

(Courtesy National Archives)

Unfortunately, the ugly event made social recovery impossible. The Sioux majority now looked at the elopement and shooting as a shameful event, and Crazy Horse's jealous detractors successfully lobbied the Oglala's elders into taking action. Crazy Horse was stripped of his shirt-wearer designation in a futile attempt to diminish his influence.

The cry of "Crazy Horse is coming" would gain even more strength in the years that followed, but the effects of the No Water mess created lasting divisions among the Sioux that would figure prominently on the day of his death.

No Water's attempt to kill The Strange Man of the Oglala did not alter his unique personality. But the loss of Black Buffalo Woman effectively ended his romantic obsession and less than a year later he wed a young Sioux woman named Black Shawl. Not long after, she gave birth to their first and only child, a girl named They Are Afraid Of Her.

When his daughter was three, Crazy Horse returned from a long raid against the Crow and was told that They Are Afraid Of Her was dead. The sickness the Whites called cholera had taken her. Black Shawl, her hair hacked off, her arms and legs gashed, was still grieving. She told him that because the village had been on the move They Are Afraid Of Her's scaffold was now far away.

Crazy Horse rode for two days before finding her bundled body on the open plain near enemy territory. As a warrior in his thirties he fully understood and accepted the prominent role of death in life, but seeing the end of his daughter, her precious playthings attached to her corpse, prompted a wave of grief that kept him at the scaffold. Ignoring hunger and thirst, he slept under the body for days, leaving only when grief had subsided enough to allow him to travel.

✤

EVEN THROUGH THE HORRORS OF COMBAT, family deaths, and the inexplicable vitriol hurled at him by cliques among his own tribe, Crazy Horse's allegiance to his people carried him forward. He fought for them with more fervor than ever.

In June of 1876 he defeated a force of almost fifteen hundred soldiers under General George Crook and led the warriors who overran Custer's command at the Greasy Grass.

By winter of the same year, the United States' icy shock at the slaughter on the Little Big Horn had defrosted into a torrent of rage that sent thousands of soldiers onto the northern Plains to deal deathblows to the Sioux and Cheyenne.

Those who were threatened or attacked, whether Sioux or Cheyenne, fled straight for Crazy Horse. All winter he defended the Sioux and their allies with a power only he could summon.

The fighting continued into the next year with painfully mixed results. Battling all winter had worn the warriors and their resources down to nothing, yet they had not been defeated. Many had gone into the reservation, but Crazy Horse was still out and so was Sitting Bull. In early spring of 1877 the heart of the Sioux Nation was still beating.

With its mission still unaccomplished, the military and its political counterparts were coming under increasing fire for not closing the case. Some were saying that it had already cost taxpayers a million dollars per dead Indian.

As public sentiment drifted once again toward an end to fighting, General George Crook, whose reputation for honesty and fairness was greater than any other White in uniform, concocted a peaceful solution. Sitting Bull and his people had crossed the border and settled in Canada, leaving Crazy Horse the sole impediment to resolution. What if Crazy Horse and his people were offered a reservation on land of his choosing? Free choice had never been a factor in the reservation process. Perhaps it would induce him to surrender.

Crook's plan was strongly opposed by his peers in the campaign because it would deny them the prestige of ending a war of decades. But, after passing through the normal convoluted channels, force in the field was momentarily suspended and Crook's initiative was given approval.

Painful as it was for Crazy Horse and his people, capitulation was unavoidable. They had fought the Whites for many months and now, exhausted and hungry, they were facing the first summer in their long history without buffalo to sustain them.

Crazy Horse accepted Crook's offer, and in May of 1877, he led eight hundred people to a site near Camp Robinson in the extreme northwestern corner of Nebraska. The arrival was made with warriors fully armed and singing songs that inspired bravery. Their heads were high, and the coming in bore no resemblance to a surrender.

Sadly, the exhibition of courage only agitated the cauldron of chaos Crazy Horse and his people had unwittingly entered—chaos they were not equipped to handle. The Sioux reservation had thrown feuding bands into close proximity. The established leaders were those who cooperated most with Whites, and the reservation was saturated with corruption that quickly infected many Indian residents.

⊰⊷⊱✕⊰⊷⊱

THE COMING OF CRAZY HORSE ignited a multitude of smoldering elements into flame. Fellow Sioux already operating in the system viewed him as a two-way threat; a menace to their own power and a wrench of unpredictability flying toward the already shaky footing of Indian demand versus government supply.

For similar reasons Whites viewed the arrival of the Sioux's greatest inspiration with apprehension. No concrete plan was in place, but the highest White figures involved agreed in general that Crazy Horse's influence could not be tolerated. His spiritual link to his followers was unbreakable, and how to interact with the man himself posed a quandary.

The social heat rose all summer fed by a continuous flow of rumor and innuendo about Crazy Horse's activities.

When a buffalo hunt was organized for his people, another Sioux leader objected to a newcomer receiving special favors; after much wrangling, the hunt was canceled.

A breakout of the Nez Perce tribe in the north led the government to the idea of raising an army of Sioux scouts to pursue the renegades. Crazy Horse was consulted. The interpreter, a half-breed with strong ties to other leaders, lied in saying that Crazy Horse had expressed a desire to kill as many Whites as possible. Although The Strange Man denied making such a statement, the suspicion and misunderstanding that evolved from the lie endured.

The scouting expedition was abandoned amidst more rumors that Crazy Horse, disarmed and all but dismounted, was planning for war.

General Crook was called to Camp Robinson to convene a council in hope that calm could be instituted, but Crazy Horse did not answer the summons. There was too much false talk in the air, and he no longer wanted contact with Crook. Over many months the General's promise that Crazy Horse would have a reservation of his choosing had gone unfulfilled.

The general organized a force and rode toward the big Sioux village to confront Crazy Horse; however, on the way, an agent of Red Cloud intercepted Crook, this agent being a venerable Sioux chief who had long been at odds with Crazy Horse. The emissary was No Water, and he had a fabrication for Crook, which was that Crazy Horse was planning to kill the general.

Crook bought the story whole and turned around. Back at Camp Robinson, he organized a thousand men to take the field, capture Crazy Horse, and bring him in. The plan (obviously pre-formulated) involved the solo captive being sent to Omaha, Nebraska, where connections could be made for transport to Florida. From there he was to be taken across the waters of the Caribbean to a cluster of treeless, windswept islands called the Dry Tortugas where he would be held indefinitely.

The huge, combined arrest force of soldiers and Sioux from Red Cloud's agency arrived at Crazy Horse's village to find that he and Black Shawl had ridden to Spotted Tail's reservation fifty miles away.

The arresting force went in pursuit and on arrival was told by Spotted Tail that his nephew was now under his protection and could not be harmed.

That night Crazy Horse talked to Spotted Tail, a trusted friend named Touch The Cloud, and a young army lieutenant who was the agency's government representative.

He said that threats to go on the warpath, to murder Crook, and all the other rumors were concoctions created by his enemies. The lieutenant suggested that Crazy Horse travel to Camp Robinson and make the same statements to the camp commander.

The next day, September 5, 1877, Crazy Horse rode to the army base, escorted by hundreds of his followers as well as the curious.

When he reached Camp Robinson, thousands were waiting. Included among them were pro- and anti-Crazy Horse factions swirling about in a lit-fuse atmosphere.

While Crazy Horse waited, the young agency lieutenant went to the commander's office and explained the reasons for the famed warrior's appearance. The colonel in charge told him it was too late for meetings. The order was that Crazy Horse be arrested and taken into custody.

Several soldiers and designated Indian police walked Crazy Horse to a windowless, log structure not far away.

As he stepped inside, the smell of feces and urine poured into his nose and he saw shackles on the walls. He was in the guardhouse.

Ripping away from his escort, Crazy Horse pulled a knife and slashed his way back to the entrance. A Sioux named Little Big Man grabbed his arms, but Crazy Horse spun again, going backward through the doorway as soldiers rushed forward. The voice of an officer called out in the midst of the struggle, "Stab the son of a bitch."

A soldier drove his bayonet into Crazy Horse's backside. The blade sliced through a kidney, releasing the toxins within as Crazy Horse went down. Lying on the ground, he made a plea:

"Let me go my friends, you have hurt me enough."

He was carried through the turbulent crowd to Doctor Valentine McGillycuddy's office. The post surgeon ordered him laid out on a cot, but Crazy Horse preferred the wooden planking of the floor because it was closer to the earth.

McGillycuddy and Touch The Cloud stayed with him until near midnight when he breathed his last.

He led the victors in the only war America has lost; but not long after, Red Cloud became one of those who saw the writing on the wall, submitting himself and his followers to the reservation. Like General Crook, he viewed Crazy Horse as a threat and treated him as such. When he died near age ninety, many Sioux still viewed him as a man who had sold out to Whites.
(Courtesy Nebraska State Historical Society)

When Crazy Horse tried to flee surprise confine-
ment it was Little Big Man who jumped him from
behind and briefly pinned his arms to his sides.
The momentary delay allowed a soldier to position
himself for a backstabbing. And it fulfilled a
prophetic vision that Crazy Horse could only be
harmed by his own people.
(Courtesy Brigham Young University)

In the morning, Worm and his wife carried their son's body away from the camp and placed it high in a large tree where it lay in state for several days. Thousands of people paid their respects.

Under cover of darkness the family took the body down and transported it to a secret location where it was entombed. Despite repeated attempts over more than a hundred years by historians and archeologists to find it, the site of Crazy Horse's mortal remains is still unknown.

But for those who know anything of him, Crazy Horse's spirit of strength, courage, generosity, and individualism lives on.

No churches are named after him, nor is he formally worshipped, but many place him on the same plane occupied by the prophets and gods of history. To the sentient of all races, the simple fact of Crazy Horse's existence confirms that divinity can be found in human form.

RECOMMENDED READING:
Crazy Horse by Mari Sandoz, Bison Books

CHAPTER TWELVE

Last Gasp

1890 SITTING BULL AND THE VARIOUS BANDS aligned with him spent more than two bloodless years in Canada. The Canadian government viewed them with respect, and Sitting Bull formed many solid relationships with a variety of officials.

But they could not stay. The buffalo were scarce, and Canada had no authority or inclination to make Sitting Bull's Sioux wards of the state.

At the same time, returning to America was an option fraught with doubt.

Sitting Bull was highly representative of the people he served. Not only had he endured years of unremitting lies and deception on the part of Whites, he had seen his nation fall from a seat of enormous power to scattered, hungry, and dispirited bands such as his own. War had depleted warriors to the point where they were unable to pose enough force to make an enemy think twice.

Even more daunting was what would happen should they return, a question for which no one had an answer. Exercising revenge for heinous offences was a staple of Sioux culture, and the majority of the people in Canada had been with Sitting Bull at the Little Big Horn. It was possible the Whites would execute them or, just as bad, put them in locked cages.

One of Sitting Bull's encampments after his return from self-imposed exile in Canada. (Courtesy Denver Public Library)

As a shining example of Indian leadership, Sitting Bull has never died. In youth he counted more than fifty coups in battle but late in his warriorhood a severe leg wound took him out of action for good and he assumed a position of spiritual height that was commanding. Even when many would not stand for him, he never stopped standing for his people. (Courtesy National Archives)

Living in limbo was impossible, however, and in late 1880 a council was held at which Sitting Bull stated clearly that, under the impossible circumstances, anyone who wanted to take their chances in returning home could do so without being chastised for leaving.

Gall, a hero at the Little Big Horn, left for the border with a large band early in 1881, and everyone, including Sitting Bull, followed in the months to come.

Shortly after crossing over, word was received that Gall's camp had been attacked by soldiers with big guns, prompting the vaunted warrior to surrender immediately. Sitting Bull instantly turned for Canada, but before he reached the border he was informed that the attack had been a misunderstanding. A woman and a warrior were killed, but there were no other casualties. Sitting Bull was also told that the attitude at a post called Fort Buford was peacefully receptive.

Again Sitting Bull informed everyone that they were free to surrender if they desired. A large number turned south to surrender, but Sitting Bull crossed back into Canada.

The aging prophet's back and forth maneuvers were frustrating to the United States. Sitting Bull was still an immeasurable magnet for Sioux faith. So long as he was free, the soul of the Sioux would be too.

Conditions in Canada, especially the availability of food, continued to decline. Later that same year the last of the Sioux crossed over once again.

Shortly after he surrendered, Sitting Bull and his people were shipped to another post where they were ensconced for more than two years as prisoners of war.

The captive status embittered Sitting Bull, but the time he spent as a P.O.W. provided surprising progress in his interaction with Whites. There is no photograph of Sitting Bull that does not reflect the intense resolve that accurately defines his character. But there was far more to the Sioux chief than determination to preserve his people, and most Whites who came to know him made unabashed expressions of admiration for the whole man.

Though he became friends with officials, service workers, and representatives of pro-Indian agencies, the most intimate early connections he made were with soldiers—in particular young, educated officers whose minds were open to cultures unlike their own.

At last, the government decided on a permanent place for Sitting Bull and his followers. In 1883 they were shipped to the Standing Rock Reservation in northern South Dakota.

Simultaneously, a new agent named James McLaughlin was assigned to the reservation. In the long, sordid history of Indian agents, McLaughlin stands out as one of the worst that ever existed. He was wholly committed to following the government line in maintaining order, a position that meshed tidily with his coldly dictatorial nature.

Stripping his clients of power topped McLaughlin's agenda, and he set about at once to execute it. He began by arbitrarily designating as chiefs only those who mindlessly did his bidding. At the same time he organized a Sioux police force, mounting and arming men who promised to follow his orders. The status of men like Sitting Bull was ignored.

Dividing the Sioux made dismantling their culture much easier, but for all his effort McLaughlin was frustrated for years, especially by his arch-nemesis, Sitting Bull. What McLaughlin missed was that no matter how much denigration was heaped on Sitting Bull, the power he held could not be diminished. Leaders from every Sioux reservation constantly sought out the sage counsel that only Sitting Bull could provide.

For seven years the cold war between the Sioux leader and the government agent went on unabated. They clashed on every initiative. Though there were victories on both sides during this time, differences between the two were never resolved. Mutual enmity was the only thing that grew from their continuous contact.

Sitting Bull's difficulties with the man he called White Hair were temporarily suspended when he signed a four month contract to appear in Buffalo Bill's Wild West Show. He was hesitant to commit, despite the money and notoriety being offered. His few previous public appearances had drawn boos and hisses from audiences, but when he discovered that he would be appearing with a young White woman he knew and admired, the incredibly gifted Annie Oakley, he signed the agreement.

The Wild West Show was America's (and the world's) premiere entertainment extravaganza, and once again Sitting Bull was cast as a villain. American audiences responded to his presence with derision, but that did not lessen Sitting Bull's attractiveness as a star of the show.

When the mammoth program crossed the border into Canada the reception of Sitting Bull changed dramatically. Known to the Canadians for astute statesmanship, wisdom, and a symbol of all that was positive about Indians, he was cheered instead of jeered.

Demand for his photos and autographs was high, and Sitting Bull enjoyed the attention. He was also buoyed by interaction with many of the show's performers and members of the public. Buffalo Bill Cody himself found much to admire in the resolute chief, and a connection of respect and trust was formed between them.

For Sitting Bull, however, performing in Cody's show was nothing more than a brief diversion. When the short contract expired, he returned to his real role as a defender of his now impoverished people.

Despite Sitting Bull's determination, hopelessness steadily rose. Adequate food was never provided and remained a constant issue. Promised resources that would provide opportunity for growth in farming and ranching were chronically absent. Corruption among various contractors was a constant. Health care and education were provided by a skimpy cadre of earnest, self-sacrificing American men and women who received next to nothing in financial and spiritual support from their own government.

During a brief stint with the Wild West Show, Sitting Bull was billed as a villain, William Cody as a star. Long afterward both men were still on good terms. (Courtesy Denver Public Library)

Behind the scenes, powerful agencies, politicians, and commercial interests, acting in collusion, worked aggressively to circumvent treaty agreements to obtain access and exploitation of lands ceded to Indian nations. With empty stomachs and full despair, the Sioux and other tribes, incarcerated behind invisible reservation bars, watched helplessly as White Americans absconded with the earthly holdings they possessed.

By the late 1880s incessant malnutrition had made Indians vulnerable to White disease. Measles, flu, and whooping cough ravaged their numbers. Something had to give; in 1888 a sudden and fantastic development took place that would drive a final nail into the coffin of traditional Indian life.

In far away Nevada, a Paiute man named Wovoka (he had been raised as Jack Wilson by a White couple with the same surname) had a compelling vision. While suffering from a high fever, an eclipse of the sun had taken place, and Wovoka revealed that he had risen from the mortal world and visited heaven. Much of Wovoka's life had been distinguished by the gift of prophecy, and he was neither fraudulent nor manipulative. The story of what he had seen swept through the broken-hearted tribes like a storm.

He had seen the Creator and all those who had died. They were happy and at peace. The Paiute prophet returned to earth with instructions on how to resurrect the past, bring the dead and the buffalo back, and rid the world of Whites. Dancing and chanting five successive nights and repeating it as often as possible would put an end to despair and suffering.

Hopeful delegations from many Plains tribes made the long trek to check out the prophet and returned with multitudes of impassioned, convincing, and outlandish stories of dead buffalo and human alike coming to life.

Everyone began to dance. Knowing the reactionary nature of Whites, the Sioux and other tribes created apparel dubbed "Ghost Shirts" that they believed would deflect the violence many feared.

The White response was sadly predictable. Though the Sioux were virtually disarmed and dismounted, malnutrived and depopulated, White authority recoiled with worry when the Sioux began to dance.

In many cases there was full scale panic. At the two largest Sioux reservations to the south, agents, especially the supremely unqualified man at Pine Ridge, began

The Prophet Wovoka (Courtesy National Archives)

Because of its fervor and hoped for results Ghost Dancing was viewed by the majority of Whites as terrorist behavior and thousands of soldiers were dispatched, primarily into Sioux country, to shut it down. The foray ended with a massacre of hungry, mostly unarmed people who had already agreed to resume reservation life. (Courtesy Denver Public Library)

to bombard Washington, D.C., saying that the fervor of the dancing was fully out of control and only the presence of troops could subdue it.

Convinced that the people they had conquered so brutally had to be whipped into submission again, the U.S. government handed the reins of control to the army, which immediately deployed thousands of troops to quash the dancing.

The Sioux panicked. More than two thousand ran off the big reserves in the south and headed for sanctuary in the Badlands of South Dakota.

The army had asked the reservation agents for lists of troublemakers they could arrest and confine. But due to the great depletion of influential warriors, the lists were small. A single, prominent name topped those James McLaughlin compiled at Standing Rock: Sitting Bull.

After years of futility in trying to render him impotent, McLaughlin finally had an opportunity to silence his nemesis for good. But the army's leaders temporarily stifled

A letter sent to Major James McLaughlin from his informant, John Carignan. The letter details Sitting Bull's activities and offers advice on strategy for his arrest. (Courtesy National Archives)

McLaughlin's murderous intent by recruiting Buffalo Bill Cody to approach Sitting Bull, convince him to give up, and arrest him if necessary.

Since the dancing had begun McLaughlin had repeatedly stated that he was in complete control, and aside from arresting Sitting Bull, no action needed to be taken. When Cody arrived to execute his mission, however, McLaughlin told Sitting Bull's friend that the dancing (now centered near the chief's sparse headquarters) had created an atmosphere of tremendous danger and advised him not to go. Cody replied that not only would he go but that he would do so without police or troops. He would be accompanied by a handful of friends and a wagonload of presents.

McLaughlin pursued his tack with the help of a co-conspirator, the commander of a nearby fort, who sent several groups of officers to call on Cody and get him drunk the night before he departed for Sitting Bull's humble cabin near the Grand River. Cody drank them all under the table and left on time the next morning.

McLaughlin and his henchmen tried one more ploy. An interpreter was dispatched to intercept Cody and tell him that Sitting Bull was already on his way in to the agency. A trail purported to be Sitting Bull's had been fabricated, and Cody fell for the deception. He turned back.

McLaughlin had been lobbying his superiors furiously, saying over and over that his own Indian police (with the backing of U.S. soldiers) were the most logical, effective, and non-violent entity to make the arrest. His entreaties were pure lies.

The Indian police were little more than McLaughlin's personal bully squad, and the animosity they held for Sitting Bull and vice versa could not have been more pronounced. The prophet considered the police nothing more than White puppets, and the Lakota police, now wholly dependent on the government, looked at the venerable leader as an outdated hindrance to their own progress down the White man's road.

McLaughlin was given the approval to use his private force to make the arrest. The stage was set for murder, and when Sitting Bull requested permission to travel south to Pine Ridge and see the Ghost Dancing, McLaughlin pulled the trigger on his lethal plan.

⊱✦⊰

BACKED BY AMERICAN TROOPS, waiting in reserve a few miles off, forty Sioux police (some of them inebriated) surrounded Sitting Bull's cabin in the darkness of pre-dawn on December 15, 1890.

More than a hundred loyalists were camped in the vicinity. They arrived in large numbers at the same time several officers burst into the cabin to rouse wives and children while taking the patriarch into custody.

On New Year's Day 1891 burial contractors piled frozen Indian dead into wagons and dumped them into mass graves while members of the Seventh Cavalry looked on. (Courtesy Denver Public Library)

ABOVE: *A large crowd attended the funerals of Indian Police killed during the assassination of Sitting Bull. The burial of the unsinkable Hunkpapa leader was attended by a handful, the majority being gravediggers. No Indians were there.* (Courtesy Denver Public Library) BELOW: *Big Foot fled for his life, as did thousands of followers when the army converged to stop the dancing. The most commonly seen photograph of him is as he lay dead on the frozen prairie at Wounded Knee, his uplifted arms stiff from the cold.* (Courtesy Denver Public Library)

Sitting Bull was pulled from his bed without resistance. With an Indian officer on each side and one directly behind he was led outside. As he came into the early morning he saw his agitated die-hard supporters and called out for help. One of the officers next to him was shot. As he fell, the wounded man fired into Sitting Bull's side. A second later, the policeman directly behind him fired a bullet into the back of Sitting Bull's head, killing him instantly.

Both sides opened up. As the firefight commenced, the Indian police were unnerved by a horse Sitting Bull had received from William Cody when he left the Wild West Show. At the sound of gunfire the equine performer sat back on its haunches, raised a hoof and pawed the air, leading the police to believe that Sitting Bull's spirit had entered the animal.

McLaughlin's squad of Indian lawmen streamed into Sitting Bull's cabin where they returned fire at the chief's followers surrounding them. Inside, they found Sitting Bull's seventeen-year-old son, Crowfoot, hiding behind a curtain and executed him.

When the White cavalry arrived, Sitting Bull's defenders scattered without firing a shot. Following their retreat, a number of White soldiers and many of the Indian police looted the premises, taking all that the old chief possessed.

The bodies of the dead, including Sitting Bull's, were piled into a wagon and taken to the nearest military post. Two days later, the dead police were elaborately interred with the entire fort in attendance.

Sitting Bull was put into the ground at the fort cemetery with no one present but his coffin builders and a handful of curious onlookers.

Many of his supporters had fled south to the Badlands where they hooked up with a leader named Big Foot. He had been leading several hundred Sioux in a wild flight for any kind of refuge. Epidemic disease, starvation, and the sudden appearance of thousands of soldiers charged with stopping the Ghost Dance had made them run, and news of Sitting Bull's assassination increased fear for their lives.

Several different army units finally caught up with Big Foot at the edge of the Badlands near the border between South Dakota and Nebraska. In the weeks they had been off the reservation, no Whites had been attacked and no goods stolen.

The military, ironically, was composed largely of the Seventh Cavalry, five of its officers being survivors of the Little Big Horn. Nearly five hundred troops moved the less than three hundred fifty Indians (only about a hundred were warriors) to a creek called Wounded Knee.

With nothing to eat, nowhere to go, and Big Foot incapacitated by severe pneumonia, the refugees had decided to return to the agency.

But it was too late.

∽⬦⬦✕⬦⬦∼

ON THE FREEZING MORNING of December 29, 1890, surrounded by White soldiers and with four cannons trained on their lodges, the warriors were ordered to come out and sit. Then they were instructed to return to their homes, twenty at a time, and bring out their weapons. The few antique or barely operative rifles and guns that appeared were not considered enough, and troops were dispatched to ransack the tipis for arms.

Women and children inside began to wail and call out, alarming the already nervous warriors sitting outside. As tensions rose a Medicine Man named Yellow Bird began to blow on an eagle bone whistle, reminding his fellow Sioux that those wearing Ghost Shirts were invulnerable to enemy bullets.

A single shot was suddenly fired from the cluster of warriors by a young Sioux man known for his mental instability.

Every army cannon, handgun, and rifle returned fire.

How many of Big Foot's people were able to escape that day is unknown. Four wounded warriors and fewer than fifty injured women and children made it to medical aid. Bodies of several hundred Sioux, two-thirds of them women and children, were strewn for miles along Wounded Knee Creek.

A blizzard descended, and after it passed, the army returned to the site of the slaughter on New Year's Day, 1891. The frozen dead who had not been retrieved by friends or relatives were gathered up and tossed into mass graves after being stripped of their Ghost Shirts, each a highly-prized souvenir.

The large killing was immediately questioned, and hearings were convened, which found several members of the Seventh Cavalry (including their commander) guilty of inappropriate conduct. The conclusions were quickly overturned by higher authority.

Years later many White eyewitnesses testified publicly and privately that as soon as the shooting started the majority of the Seventh Cavalry went berserk, chasing down

and killing every Indian they could find regardless of age, gender, or lack of armament.

The only official, federal acknowledgement of the atrocity at Wounded Knee came in bizarre form. Perhaps it was produced as a result of relief at the conclusion of frontier warfare. It might have come as a bent effort to cover guilt. Legitimacy was possible too.

Whatever the reason it was typical of America's response to being in the wrong.

Fourteen members of the Seventh Cavalry, all of whom participated in the mass killing at Wounded Knee, were singled out for America's highest military award: the Medal of Honor.

RECOMMENDED READING:

Sitting Bull's Story by Dan Diessner, Upton & Sons Publishing.

Members of the Seventh Cavalry in the field at Wounded Knee, proudly displaying the weapons that killed hundreds of women and children (Courtesy Library of Congress)

Leonard Peltier stares out a window in one of several penitentiaries he has inhabited for half his life. Wrongfully convicted of murder, he stands today for Indian people in America as a symbol of the traditional values long discarded by the 'civilized' world in its scramble for wealth. Adherence to those values has been the key to his survival through thirty years of slavery behind bars. (Courtesy Jeffry Scott)

One Last Thing

2006 WHEN THE LAST SIGNIFICANT BAND of Comanche surrendered its warriors, they were penned in a high, roofless stockade. At feeding time a wagon filled with raw beef would pull up outside the enclosure and soldiers would lob meat over the wall.

Today, goods are still being lobbed onto reservations from a distance by the people of the United States. Indian jewelry is bought and worn, Indian names are attached to businesses and products, and institutionalized gambling draws money from multitudes.

The thousands of people living on reservations, however, are ignored except when the potential for commercial exploitation of their holdings arises. Their blood is praised far and wide, but their lives are avoided, and the logic and beauty of their traditional culture has never been investigated by appreciable numbers of Americans.

From the time the armed insurgency of their ancestors ended they have been left to rot as nobodies, flailing for purpose in life.

For decades after they stopped fighting, the government predicated Indian policy on the assumption their charges would become extinct. But even after it became clear that Indians would not die out, America continued its longstanding approach of aggressive and premeditated neglect.

This policy has helped make thousands of Indian people a disproportionate part of the more than two million Americans currently in cages throughout the country.

The most prominent Indian convict's current incarceration is consistent with the lawless treatment of his antecedents. Leonard Peltier's trial for the alleged killing of two FBI Agents in 1975 stands as the greatest contemporary example of injustice applied to an Indian individual. Innocence or guilt was rendered irrelevant by the rank manipulation of the American justice system by an amoral triad of law enforcement, prosecutors, and judges. Like Satanta and Spotted Tail before him, Peltier sits in a cell by virtue of resistance, not proven guilt. He is now nearing thirty years behind bars.

All this from the "greatest nation on earth," which adopted the actions it took toward American Indians in the nineteenth century as a model of behavior toward people of different beliefs in the twentieth century and beyond.

The United States will never live up to its glorified billing as a beacon for humanity so long as it refuses to legitimately recognize and respect other cultures, starting with the Indian citizens living within its borders today.

RECOMMENDED READING:

In the Spirit of Crazy Horse, by Peter Matthiessen, Viking

[INDEX]